ROMAN CATHOLIC CLAIMS

ROMAN CATHOLIC CLAIMS

BY

CHARLES GORE, M.A., D.D. (Edin.)
OF THE COMMUNITY OF THE RESURRECTION
CANON OF WESTMINSTER

SEVENTH EDITION

WIPF & STOCK · Eugene, Oregon

Wipf and Stock Publishers
199 W 8th Ave, Suite 3
Eugene, OR 97401

Roman Catholic Claims
By Gore, Charlles
ISBN 13: 978-1-60608-117-4
Publication date 8/27/2008
Previously published by Longmans, Green and Co., 1900

PREFACE TO THE SIXTH EDITION

A GOOD deal of controversy on the questions in dispute between England and Rome has gone on since this book was first issued. On our side admirable work has been done by Dr. Bright in his various publications; by Fr. Puller in his *Primitive Saints and the See of Rome*, and in his recent examination of the Bull *Apostolicae Curae*, by Mr. Denny and Mr. Lacey in the *De hierarchia Anglicana* and by Mr. Wakeman in his *History of the Church of England*. Work of this quality and thoroughness might seem to render quite unnecessary the greater part of this little book. But in fact—presumably because it presents in a brief compass a review of the whole question—it still continues in some demand. It has now again become necessary to reprint it, and in doing so it has seemed better not to alter substantially the book as it has stood hitherto, but to add some supplementary matter. Accordingly, a chapter (XI) on recent papal utterances has been added, and some appended notes, especially one consisting of a paper which was read this year at the Church Congress, dealing with the application to theology of the idea of development.

In another book (*Dissertations*; John Murray) I have had occasion to examine at some length the Roman doctrine of Transubstantiation, and I may say here, that the more closely it is examined *in its origins* the more convinced one becomes that it violates altogether the analogy of the doctrine of the Incarnation and the accompanying principle that the supernatural does not destroy the natural. Later Roman theology has gone some way towards evacuating the term of its legitimate meaning by affirming that each consecrated species is still 'something objectively real'—that is, a substance in the only sense in which a meaning is now assigned to the word; but in the original signification of transubstantiation, in the sense in which it became a dogma of the Roman Church, and as seen in some of its permanent practical consequences, it embodies a disastrous principle.[1]

Outside our own communion, we owe a special debt of gratitude to a group of foreign theologians who have given candid examination to our Anglican ordinal with very favourable results. And the *Answer of the Greek Church of Constantinople to the Papal Encyclical on Unity* (obtainable of the Very Rev. Archimandrite Eustathius Metellinos, Priest of the Greek Church of the Annunciation in Manchester) is a sure sign that the Eastern protest against Rome is as inflexible as it is well grounded in fact.

C. G.

CHRISTMAS 1896.

---

[1] See *Dissertations*, p. 284.

FROM THE PREFACES TO FORMER EDITIONS

IT is always important to explain what exactly is assumed at starting in every book, or in other words, for what class of readers it is written. This book then is written for persons who accept, or are disposed to accept, the Catholic position; that is, who believe that Christ instituted a visible Church, and intended the apostolic succession of the ministry to form at least one necessary link of connection in it: who accept the Catholic Creeds and the declared mind of the Church as governing their belief: and who believe in the sacraments, as celebrated by a ministry of apostolic authority in its different grades, as the covenanted channels or instruments of grace. Further, this book is addressed to catholic-minded persons who are members of the Church of England, or Churches in communion with her. Such persons find themselves attacked from the side of Rome, and hear it denied that it is possible to be Catholics without being Roman Catholics. It is against such claims made upon us from the side of the Roman Church that the following pages are intended to be a defence, mostly in the way of explaining positively the Anglican position, and showing it to be both Catholic and rational. For the Roman Catholic claims may be dealt with by those who cannot accept them, in one of two ways. They may be examined and shown to be in themselves in conflict with history, and untenable. This has been often done. It was done with immense effect by "Janus" in *The Pope and the Council*.[1] It is hard to imagine how any one can fail to perceive the crushing force of this work. Once again it has been done recently by Dr. Salmon, Provost of Trinity College, Dublin, in his *Infallibility of the Church*.[2] As a *destructive* effort this book also seems conclusive.

But there is another method of dealing with the Roman claim. It is by strengthening the fabric of a positive Catholicity, which is not Roman. Such a defensive method it has been my aim to follow in this book. So far as attack is a necessary part of defence, it has not been possible to avoid it. But my purpose is positive, not negative—to build, not to destroy.

I believe, with a conviction the strength of which I could hardly express, that it is the vocation of the English Church to realize and to offer to mankind a Catholicism which is Scrip-

[1] Authorised English Trans.; Rivingtons, 1869.
[2] London: John Murray, 1888.

tural, and represents the whole of Scripture: which is historical, and can know itself free in face of historical and critical science; which is rational and constitutional in its claim of authority, free at once from lawlessness and imperialism. That the English Church for her many sins will need the purification of much discipline and suffering before she can in any adequate measure realize her vocation, cannot be doubted. There will be trials calculated to test the loyalty of the staunchest hearts: but only through such trials is any great vocation realized. And those who continue with the Church of England in her temptations have surely appointed to them a position and a work of privilege and fruitfulness in the kingdom of Christ.

It was then in the belief that no labour is lost which goes to strengthen the fabric of the English Church, and enable her to realize with security her catholic polity and life, that this book was written (in 1888), and has been several times corrected and amplified. My aim has been throughout to write not as "a member of the High Church party," but as a loyal son of the Church of England. Even the secular newspapers seem to be coming to recognize that real acceptance of Church of England principles forces a man to realize his profound debt to that Tractarian revival, which, starting from a small and organized band of workers, sufficiently compact to be called a party in a right sense, has leavened so largely the whole life of the Church as to make the phrase "the High Church *party*" somewhat anachronistic. I have endeavoured to write then simply as a Churchman, Catholic and English, owing no narrower subjection than these words involve.

Thus Chapter I. is a general explanation of the Anglican position as the "*via media*," and a general statement of our attitude towards the Roman Church. After that follows an answer in detail to each article of the Roman assault. Thus Chapter II. vindicates the Anglican or Catholic conception of Church unity as against the Roman modification of it. Chapter III. endeavours to explain the true or primitive conception of Church authority, and Chapter IV. the true relation of the Church to the Bible. Chapter V. examines the Roman interpretation of our Lord's promise to St. Peter. Chapters VI. and VII. bring to the test of history the modern claims of the Roman see. Chapter VIII. expounds the meaning of schism, and clears the English Church from the charge of it. Chapter IX. is occupied in vindicating the validity and jurisdiction of the Anglican episcopate; and Chapter X. in defending the Anglican Church on the charge of heresy.

C. G.

CONTENTS

CHAP.		PAGE
I.	THE *VIA MEDIA* AND THE ROMAN CATHOLIC DEVELOPMENT,	1
II.	THE UNITY OF THE CHURCH,	25
III.	THE AUTHORITY OF THE CHURCH AND THE DEVELOPMENT OF DOCTRINE,	37
IV.	THE BIBLE IN THE CHURCH,	60
V.	THE PROMISE TO ST. PETER,	75
VI.	THE GROWTH OF THE ROMAN CHURCH,	93
VII.	THE DEVELOPMENT OF THE PAPACY IN LATIN CHRISTIANITY,	106
VIII.	THE NATURE OF SCHISM,	125
IX.	ANGLICAN ORDINATIONS,	141
X.	ANGLICAN ORTHODOXY,	168
XI.	THREE RECENT PAPAL UTTERANCES,	185

APPENDED NOTES.

I. THE BEARING OF THE THEORY OF DEVELOPMENT ON CHRISTIAN DOCTRINE, ... 203

II. THE CONCEPTION OF CHURCH UNITY IN ST. HILARY, ... 211

III. ST. BASIL AND ST. HILARY ON DOCTRINAL CONFUSION IN THE CHURCH, ... 212

IV. THE COMMON DIFFUSION OF THE SCRIPTURES AMONG CHRISTIANS OF THE EMPIRE, . . 213

V. THE DOUBTS AS TO THE DOCUMENT ON ABYSSINIAN ORDINATIONS, ... 214

CHAPTER I.

THE *VIA MEDIA* AND THE ROMAN CHURCH.

THE English Churchman is constantly liable to be told—and to be told from very opposite quarters—that if he were only 'logical' he would join the Roman Church: that belief in a visible Church and in its authority, in the apostolic succession, and the jurisdiction of the episcopate, leads legitimately and logically to the conclusion of submitting to the see of Rome.[1] Thus Anglicanism is represented as an impossible *via media* between pure Protestantism and Rationalism on the one hand and Roman Catholicism on the other.

We are perhaps a little encouraged to meet these claims made in the name of logic with a good heart by the consideration that logic, in the sense of argument, is apt to be most efficacious when it is most one-sided, and content to ignore everything in the facts which does not suit its case. "Reason" it has been most wisely said "is wide, and manifold, and waits its time; and argument is partial, one-sided, and often then most effective, when least embarrassed by seeing too much."[2]

[1] This is the argument not only of Roman controversialists but also of Dr. Hatch in his reply to Dr. Liddon *Contemporary Review* June 1885, p. 864. In fact, as is pointed out on p. 124— the theory of the Papacy involves a quite different principle from that of the Episcopate. See also an excellent argument in *The Guardian* of May 15, 1889, p. 758.
[2] Church *Human Life and its Conditions* p. 85.

The most plain case is by no means always the most true. Thus Hooker remarks about the early heresies on the Incarnation that "because this divine mystery is more true than plain, divers having framed the same to their own conceits and fancies are found in their expositions thereof more plain than true." So in effect in the early centuries it was the heretics who were notorious for one-sided appeals to 'logic,' while the Church was for this very reason called the 'via media' because she held on her way between opposite extremes, persisting in holding together a complex scriptural idea or truth which one-sided heresies would have torn asunder.[1]

---

[1] This has been drawn out by Professor Mozley in a passage which has become famous: see *The Theory of Development* pp. 41-43: "In this way the logical controversy proceeded on the great doctrines of Christianity in the first centuries: different sects developed these in their own way; and each sect appealed triumphantly to the logical irresistibleness of its development. The Arian, the Nestorian, the Apollinarian, the Eutychian, the Monothelite developments, each began with a great truth, and each professed to demand one, and only one, treatment for it. All successively had one watchword, and that was, 'Be logical.' Be logical, said the Arian: Jesus Christ is the Son of God; a son cannot be coeval with his father. Be logical, said the Nestorian: Jesus Christ was man and was God; he was therefore two persons. Be logical, said the Apollinarian: Jesus Christ was not two persons; he was not, therefore, perfect God and perfect man too. Be logical, said the Eutychian: Jesus Christ was only one person; he could therefore only have one nature. Be logical, said the Monothelite: Jesus Christ was only one person; He could therefore only have one will. Be logical, said the Macedonian: the Holy Ghost is the Spirit of the Father, and therefore cannot be a person distinct from the Father. Be logical, said the Sabellian: God is one, and therefore cannot be three. Be logical, said the Manichean: evil is not derived from God, and therefore must be an original substance independent of him. Be logical, said the Gnostic: an infinite Deity cannot really assume a finite body. Be

We have in fact no cause to be ashamed of this phrase the *via media* which common consent has fixed upon Anglicanism. It was a phrase in which the Church of old gloried as a proper description of her position. And in what sense? It did not mean the way of modera-

logical, said the Novatian: there is only one baptism for the remission of sins; there is therefore no remission for sin after baptism. Be logical, to come to later times, said the Calvinist: God predestinates, and therefore man has not free will. Be logical, said the Anabaptist: the Gospel bids us to communicate our goods, and therefore does not sanction property in them. Be logical, said the Quaker: the Gospel enjoins meekness, and therefore forbids war. Be logical, says every sect and school: you admit our premises; you do not admit our conclusions. You are inconsistent. You go a certain way and then arbitrarily stop." . . . .
"The whole dogmatic creed of the Church has been formed in direct contradiction to such apparent lines of consecutiveness. The Nestorian saw as clearly as his logic could tell him, that two persons must follow from two natures. The Monophysite saw as clearly as his logic could tell him, that one nature must follow from one person. The Arian, the Monothelite, the Manichean, saw as clearly as their logic could tell them on their respective questions, and argued inevitably and convincingly to themselves. To the intellectual imagination of the great heresiarchs of the early ages, the doctrine of our Lord's nature took boldly some one line, and developed continuously and straightforwardly some one idea; it demanded unity and consistency. The Creed of the Church, steering between extremes and uniting opposites, was a timid artificial creation, a work of diplomacy. In a sense they were right. The explanatory Creed of the Church was a diplomatic work; it was diplomatic, because it was faithful. With a shrewdness and nicety like that of some ablest and most sustained course of statecraft and cabinet policy, it went on adhering to the complex original idea, and balancing one tendency in it by another. One heresiarch after another would have infused boldness into it; they appealed to one element and another in it, which they wanted to be developed indefinitely. The Creed kept its middle course, rigidly combining opposites; and a mixed and balanced erection of dogmatic language arose."

tion, the 'middle way' of steering clear of all thorough and intelligible and free statement of principle. It meant rather the way of combination, the way of comprehension and synthesis. The Church held together what a hasty logic would have torn asunder. In 'the Word made flesh' we have a complex or double fact —a union of Godhead and manhood—and the Church had to be true to both parts of her creed, to the Divinity *and* the humanity, letting neither be ignored in the interest of the other. The same duty presented itself in regard to the doctrine of God: here again she had to maintain both God's unity as against Tritheists, and the Trinity as against Unitarians. Thus the *Quicunque vult* is a document full of balanced and antithetic clauses, just the sort of clauses which are irritating to a hasty logic. "Like as we are compelled by the Christian verity to acknowledge every Person by Himself to be God and Lord, so are we forbidden by the Catholic religion to say [what seems the 'logical' consequence] there be three Gods, or three Lords." But this principle of combination holds beyond the area of theology proper. When we are considering the function of the Church and the relation of the Church as a society to the individual, we have to guard the same principle. You may press the claims of the individual to freedom to the extent of annihilating all real unity, or you may press Church authority so as to annihilate the free development of the individual. The former extreme we call individualism, the latter imperialism or absolutism. Both are 'logical,' that is to say both are the logical application of a true principle, but they are the one-sided applications of it, and we should be inclined to call Protestantism on one side individualistic, and Romanism absolutist, on the other: while the *via media* undertakes the more difficult but not the less necessary task of preserving the balance by keeping hold of both terms. The case is just the same with authority and private judgment—it is in fact only the same problem in the intellectual sphere. The ideal state is a *via media* in which the due authority of the Church nourishes the spiritual judgment of the individual into mature life and freedom till "he that is spiritual judgeth all things yet he himself is judged of no man." The extremes are represented by a dogmatism which crushes instead of quickening the reason of the individual, making it purely passive and acquiescent, and on the other hand by an unrestrained development of the individual judgment which becomes eccentric and lawless just because it is unrestrained. If there is much of this latter extreme in modern life, there is also in the Roman Church a great deal of the former. Once again and for the last time, the life of the soul is intended to be nourished by a due correspondence between external gifts of grace, of which the sacraments are the visible channels, and the internal action of faith. Now in this case also the doctrine of the sacraments has without a doubt been preached and accepted in such a way as to lead to their being treated as charms, or substitutes for personal spiritual effort; and on the other side the sufficiency of faith has been proclaimed in a way that made men ignore the necessity of the sacraments. The mean lies in the belief both in the validity of sacramental grace and in the necessity for the responsive action of faith. Thus in all departments of religious life we come upon this principle of the *Via Media*, and the English Church may well be proud of the title. It is not indeed the case that we could reasonably claim to have realized this ideal standard with any degree of completeness : but it represents the ideal which the providence of God has made it our special responsibility to maintain, because circumstances have linked us at once to the ancient organization and authority of the Church and to the freer life and scriptural appeal of the Reformation, and have thus given us the special opportunity of showing that Church authority is not incompatible with the appeal to Scripture and to reason. We are invested to an exceptional degree with the responsibility of being true to the *whole* of the deposit of truth : of resisting the fascination of one-sided developments : and thus standing ready with the whole treasury of Christian truth unimpaired to meet the demands which a new age makes upon it with its new developments of character and circumstance.

So, speaking broadly, the complaint which we should make of the Roman Church is—not that she is heretical —nor that she does not represent a real development of principles which are truly Christian, but that she represents a one-sided development, and by this very one-sidedness has been prevented, both in our time and at the epoch of the Reformation, from expressing at all adequately the whole of Christianity, and that thus in claiming (as in fact she does claim) to be the whole, she has taken up a position which is essentially schismatic :

for that is essentially schismatic which makes for a part the claim of the whole.

Broadly, it is very easy to justify this view of the Roman Church. Each race has had in the Catholic Church its own particular function. It was the function, for instance, of the Greek race with its peculiar intellectual subtlety and philosophical power to bring out into clear light the 'treasures of wisdom' which lay hid in Christ, to grasp and enunciate the principles of the Incarnation and the Trinity—in a word, to be the theologians of the Church. In theology proper the Roman Church has been by comparison weak, but her strength lay in the gift of government. It was hers to bring out all the wealth of authority which the facts and forces of Christianity contained within their scope. The faculty of empire passed from pagan to Christian Rome transformed in purpose and motive, but fundamentally the same. In the exercise of this power lay the glory of the Papacy but also its danger. Just as the danger of Greek Christianity had been the tendency to degenerate into an aimless theological accuracy—a barren subtlety of intellectual or verbal distinctions, so the danger of Roman Christianity lay in imperialism. The whole idea of the Church becomes under her treatment in a measure secularised. The Church becomes a great world-empire for purposes of spiritual government and administration. Hence, for instance, the primary conception of her unity becomes that of unity of government, the sort of unity which most readily submits itself to secular tests and most naturally postulates a visible centre and head; and the dominant force in all religious questions becomes authority rather than truth. Indeed all the needs of the early mediæval period tended to add strength to this tendency. The untamed, undisciplined races which formed the material of our modern nations were subjected to the yoke of the Church (mostly at the will of kings or chiefs) as to an external law, which was to train, mould, restrain them. The one need of such an age was authoritative discipline, and the Church became largely a 'schoolmaster to bring men to Christ.' She had in fact to do with children in mind; with children whose one religious faculty, which was in full exercise, was faith, in the form of a great readiness to accept revelations of the unseen world and to respect their ministers—the sort of faith which asks for nothing but a sufficiently firm voice of authority. Christianity thus became, by a one-sided development, a great imperialist and hierarchical system. The peremptory needs of government tended to overshadow earlier conceptions of the Church's function even in relation to the truth. Compare the Roman Leo's view of the truth with that of the Alexandrian Didymus or Athanasius, and the contrast is marked. Both Easterns and Westerns insist on the importance of the Church's dogma, but to the Easterns it is the guide in the knowledge of God, to the Westerns it is the instrument to subdue and discipline the souls of men. Thus the authoritativeness of tone which becomes characteristic of the Western Church makes her impatient of the slow and complex methods of arriving at the truth on disputed points, which belonged to the earlier idea of the 'rule of faith.' The comparison of traditions, the elaborate appeal to Scripture, these methods are too slow and too indecisive : something more rapid and imperious is wanted. It is no longer enough to conceive of the Church as the catholic witness to a faith once for all delivered. She must be the living voice of God, the oracle of the Divine Will. And just as the strength and security of witness lies in the comparison and consent of independent testimonies, so the strength of authoritative oracular utterance lies in unimpeded, unqualified centrality, and Christendom needs a central chair of truth, where Divine Authority speaks and rules.

Such has been broadly the Roman development of the Christian religion. It has been a real and powerful development of principles really Christian, but a one-sided, and for this reason an incomplete development, and one which, as soon as it claims to be the whole, becomes schismatic.

That Roman Catholicism is an incomplete development is plain to us at the present time, as we look at the matter from outside, on several grounds.

(1) It is unscriptural. Scripture says a good deal about authority, and therefore there are certain passages of Scripture with which Rome is thoroughly at home— which she has thoroughly made her own. But with the whole of Scripture she is not at home. This is shown by the immense gulf between practical current Romanism and the general tone of the New Testament—a gulf which is partly the cause and partly the effect of the prevalent ignorance and disuse of Scripture, as a whole, which is notorious and admitted amongst Roman Catholics. Thus M. Henri Lasserre who has made a

name by his devotion to our Lady of Lourdes, recently published, with the imprimatur of the Archbishop of Paris and under the special benediction of the Roman Pontiff, a translation into French of the four Gospels. He did this, he tells us in his preface, on account of "a fact notorious and universal"—a fact which is regarded as "the primary cause of the diminution of the Christian spirit"—namely, that the Gospel "is very rarely read even by those who profess to be fervent Catholics. Never at all by the multitude of the faithful." "In fact," continues M. Lasserre, "ask your neighbours and your friends, all who make up your circle; ask yourself, my dear reader :—and you will not hesitate to affirm, not perhaps without a profound astonishment, that for a hundred persons who practise the sacraments, there is often not a single one who has ever opened the Gospels, except at hazard, and to go through or to meditate here and there upon a few isolated verses." Anything like continuous knowledge of the Gospels, he goes on to explain at length, simply does not exist.[1] Such a state of things Cardinal Manning appears not only to recognise as a fact, but to justify. "Catholics readily admit," he says, that "they do not go to the text of Scripture for their devotion, as others do who are out of the unity of the Church." "The Church puts into the hands of its people books of devotion which represent the whole order

---

[1] I quote from the twenty-third edition. Shortly after, this book was suppressed, on the ground of inaccuracies of translation. If this had been the only ground, we should, of course, have expected that another translation, freed from such inaccuracies, would at once have appeared with the same *imprimaturs* and benedictions. There was an obviously boundless demand for a version of the Gospels in French. [1889.]

and completeness of revelation, and not the partial and unordered aspect of Scripture."[1] Now we English Churchmen feel that there is a very natural reason why Roman Catholics should not know more than select passages of Scripture. Their favourite devotions to the blessed Virgin and the Saints, the doctrines of indulgences, and of purgatory, as commonly held amongst them, find no countenance at all in the New Testament. A man cannot be at home in the current Roman doctrine of 'good works' and in St. Paul's Epistles. And this unscripturalness of the Roman Church has a further result: we do not, we cannot, look to her for much help in interpreting the New Testament as a whole. Immense progress has been made in Scriptural interpretation within the last thirty or forty years,[2] but how singularly little has the Roman Church helped in it, or is she likely to help in it. We go to older Roman

---

[1] Manning's *Temporal Mission of the Holy Ghost* pp. 210, 211. P. 208 he speaks of "the level and dim surface of the Sacred Text." There may be eyes to which the surface of nature is level and dim; otherwise it would be inconceivable how any one could apply such epithets *e.g.* to the Epistles and Gospels.

[2] I do not, of course, mean that we should not desire in many modern commentators, and expounders of Scripture, a much greater reverence for the mind of the Church, but I do say that such commentators as Westcott, Lightfoot, Trench, or—out of Presbyterian communities — Milligan, Godet, Delitzsch, and others,—with such preachers and writers as Benson, Holland, Liddon, Keble, Church, Mozley, Pusey, and Newman (almost wholly in his Anglican days), represent for our age a really fresh and genuine drawing out of the meaning of the inspired books, and give us as a result immense help in understanding them. By the united labours of many devout spirits, Holy Scripture is being gradually made to live again. [1888.]

commentaries (such as that of Cornelius à Lapide) for accumulated information on the various opinions, good, bad, and indifferent, which have been held as to the meaning of Scripture, and sometimes for valuable suggestion : we go to Father Coleridge and others for a great deal of suggestive practical commentary on the Gospels —but for the legitimate and critical and real interpretation of the New Testament, especially of St. Paul or St. John, we look with very little hope to the Roman Church.

(2) It is unhistorical. The Roman Church has dragged along with her as a heritage of the past, from which she cannot break, a 'rule of faith' which makes a new dogma once for all equivalent to a false dogma. It has therefore been forced upon her to maintain that dogmas which have been rendered necessary by the accentuation of authority or by the exigencies of popular devotions which it was not possible or expedient to restrain, such as Papal infallibility and supremacy, the Immaculate Conception and the doctrine of Indulgences, are portions of primitive Christianity, at least in substance. This hopeless task she can only accomplish by a treatment of antiquity which is absolutely inconsistent with any honest attempt to read its record. Thus practically Roman writers deny that antiquity has a real record which we can read, and ought to read freely. Cardinal Manning says: "the appeal to antiquity (*i.e.* the appeal behind the present teaching of the Church) is both a treason and a heresy. . . . I may say in strict truth that the Church has no antiquity. It rests upon its own supernatural and perpetual consciousness. . . . The only divine evidence to us of what was primitive is the witness and voice of the Church

at this hour."[1] Roman writers generally bid us use the living voice of the Church as a witness to what the Church of the past did think, and appear to suppose the argument of the 'difficulty'[2] of reading the past records of the Church a sufficient reason for ignoring them. Thus almost the whole of their recent literature has become saturated with a spirit of unfaithfulness to historical fact. There is a great deal of Romanism in the Church from the fifth century downward, and this they produce with an excessive willingness—they have it at their fingers' ends. But we have ceased almost to hope to find in a modern Roman writer a candid review of the whole facts of a case where the Roman Claims or dogmas are in question. Candour, an attempt to fairly produce the whole case, a love of the whole truth—this seems to have vanished from their literature,

[1] *Temporal Mission*, Third ed. 1877, pp. 238-240. Elsewhere, p. 29, he calls the appeal to Scripture and antiquity whether by individuals or local Churches "essentially rationalistic." We on the other hand should hold that the Church is the primary teacher of the individual, but that her teaching, because it is Catholic and nothing more, must admit of being verified by the individual for himself, if he has adequate knowledge and patience, in the field of antiquity. Morinus' work *de Sacris Ordinationibus* is a magnificent instance of a current church doctrine in the Roman Church having been in former days altered by a free examination of the past records. See *The Church and the Ministry* p. 68, note 1.

[2] Rivington's *Authority* p. 29. P. 56 he quotes a remark of St. Francis "that the early Church," on the Protestant showing "must have had a long speaking-tube indeed to make itself audible to Luther across the centuries, without these centuries hearing what it said." Luther put his ear very little to the speaking-tube, and perhaps there was too much noise during the Reformation to make it very easy to listen to the voice, but I should have thought that the revival of the knowledge of Greek among other things was of the nature of a speaking-tube from the early centuries.

and its place is taken by an abundant skill in making the best of all that looks Romewards in Church history, and ignoring the rest. Indeed it seems to be not only in dealing with the Papal claims that the Roman Church is disqualified from dealing broadly and frankly with facts. She has adopted a fatal tone of distrust towards the critical reason altogether, so that she seems by her whole method to put herself at a disadvantage in dealing with some of the most pressing problems of our time which are coming up for solution.

For example. Some fifty years ago a very powerful attack was made on the genuineness of New Testament documents, and consequently on the historical character of the Gospel record. On the whole we can claim that this attack has been met and repulsed, and that the cause of the New Testament history and records—the authorship, for instance, of St. John's Gospel, the historical trustworthiness of the Acts of the Apostles, and the genuineness of St. Paul's and St. John's Epistles—stands now on stronger ground than ever before, in proportion as the attack was more scientific, more radical, and more searching. It has been met by men who combined with a strong faith in the Christian Creed and Scriptures a courageous belief in evidence, a fearless love of frank inquiry, and it is not therefore surprising that the victory has been won with little aid from the Roman Catholic Church. Now the attack has moved backwards, and is directed against the Old Testament. On this field the whole problem is still in solution, and the victory is still to be won. But it will be won, we are sure, by students who, on the one hand, hold with a sure confidence to the Inspiration of Scrip-

THE ROMAN CHURCH. 15

ture, and take a careful view of what the Church seems actually to have committed herself to on this subject; and, on the other hand, face with a determined boldness, and patience, and accuracy the critical problem, the evidence as it actually is. This field of controversy is still in the main before us, but the experience of the past leads us surely to expect the champions of Holy Scripture in the fray to come from some other quarter than amongst Roman theologians—for this reason, that instead of the temper required for dealing with the problem, they seem to exhibit a mixture of exaggerated dogmatism with undue scepticism as to our faculties for the discovery of truth. And it cannot be pretended that the question is one only for the learned. There is no question which more cries out for solution amongst the working classes than what they are to think about the historical truth of the whole Bible. Hitherto, certainly, the Roman Church, as it has not done much to help us on the ground of the New Testament, so again has no ready answer as to the Old. For while Cardinal Manning declares that the authoritative teaching of the Holy Catholic Church "excludes the supposition that falsehood and error can be found" in any of the Canonical books, on the other hand an able Roman layman[1] has vindicated his liberty to maintain in the

---

[1] I allude to Mr. St. George Mivart's articles in the *Nineteenth Century* of July and Dec. 1887. It does not seem as if the Roman Church was in fact more committed on this subject than our own. There is the same variety of opinion. The Vatican Council has expressly defined that the books of the Old and New Testament "have God for their author." Newman, however, *Nineteenth Century* Feb. 1884 p. 188, makes 'author' (auctor) mean no more than 'primary cause.' Most recognized Roman writers

public press an acceptance of the conclusions of 'advanced critics' on the Old Testament, and even of conclusions which would go far to undermine the historical trustworthiness of the New Testament documents.

I have been endeavouring to indicate two points in which the Roman development of Catholicity, because it is one-sided, has had the effect of maiming Christianity, and disqualifying it from dealing with some of the tasks assigned to it. The over-development of authoritativeness has led to the Roman Church becoming both unscriptural and unhistorical. Thus we Anglicans are sure that to accept the Roman Church as being the whole Catholic Church would be to betray a great trust, and to make ourselves instrumental in letting Christianity become narrowed as it comes down the ages. "There are more things" in Scripture and in Catholicism "than are dreamt of in her philosophy." The Church of the first ages was richer in possible developments of character and power than the Church of Rome.

I may then attempt to put the case of an Anglican Churchman at starting in this way:

We find ourselves by our baptism members of a Church which claims to be part of Christ's Holy Catholic Church, and which, at the same time, has become separated from the rest of Western Christendom by a refusal to submit to the claims of the see of Rome.

e.g. Cornely *Hist. et Crit. Introd. in V. T. Compendium* Paris 1889 pp. 273-278, appear to regard themselves as bound to defend the historical truth even of Judith and Tobit. [1889. The above paragraph contains an element of prophecy. For later events, and the Papal Encyclical on the subject, see Chapter XI.]

We do not find on examination that we fail to comply with any of the conditions of catholic communion which the ancient and undivided Church recognized.

We cannot in the face of history treat the present claims of the Papal see as tenable or just. In particular, the force of these claims is broken, as by an immense breakwater, by the whole Eastern Church with her millions of Catholic Christians, long before it reaches us. For history forces us to recognize in the Roman claims the main cause of the schism of East and West: it forces us to see in the Papal system a development of Christianity which is less than catholic.

On the other hand, we see in the ancient and undivided Church a coherent system of beliefs and institutions and practices, which has been continuous under the development of Rome and in the traditions of the East, and which is richer and fuller in possibilities of life than either the one or the other taken apart. To this richer and completer life of the undivided Church we make our appeal. From it we would start afresh. For while we thankfully recognize that, in God's good providence, nothing occurred in the English Reformation which broke the continuity of our Church in any essential matter with the Church of the past, it is not to the Reformation we wish to appeal so much as to antiquity. The Reformation was a time of reaction rather than of settlement. We see the 'fresh springs' of a life constantly new rather in the principles of the ancient Church and in the present power of the Holy Ghost. And to reassure us in appealing back to the undivided Church and claiming our continuity with her, God has blessed with results beyond what its first leaders would have dared to ask, the revival of religious life amongst us, which, during the last fifty years, has stirred and taken form on the basis of this very appeal. Just in proportion as the Anglican Church has been content to act as if she were Catholic, and to stir up the gifts within her, in that proportion we find she is so and has the living Spirit in her body.

What is reassuring is not merely that the faith of individuals, whether priests or people, finds its response: it is not merely that we are allowed to realise our catholicity in this or that parish, this or that institution: it is not merely that all the prophecies of evil which those who left us forty years ago ventured to utter, have been signally falsified [1]—it is true further and beyond this, that our Church is driven in her formal and corporate action more and more to take her stand on the only basis which is tenable and enduring, the basis of catholic principle. It is surely remarkable that in the Conference of Bishops of the Anglican Communion in

[1] Cf. for instance Dr. Newman's *Loss and Gain* p. 288. "They [Catholic-minded people] will keep going one by one as they ripen." . . . "Their Catholic principles lead them on, and there is nothing to drive them back." On the other hand, in the articles by the Editor of *The Month* (July 1885 p. 350), we discern a different tone after a lapse of many years, and in the light of the experience they have brought. "Their eyes [*i.e.* of those who represent the Tractarians now] are no longer turned to the city of God. . . . They are quite content with their position. Cf. Rivington *Dependence* p. 157: "Of late years this attitude [of preference for Rome] has very much disappeared. It is now taught that it is a comparative blessing to have been born in the Anglican Branch, as it is called, and not in the Roman Communion."

THE ROMAN CHURCH. 19

the year 1888, a proposal which was made (if report speaks true) subversive of the principle of the apostolic succession,[1] should not have been able to get a hearing; or be allowed to appear in the official report. It is surely remarkable how the bishops take their stand not so much on the Articles, as on the Catholic creeds and Ecumenical Councils[2]—not, that is, on a document which represents rather the best compromise which could be arrived at locally, at a time when questions were not ripe for settlement, but upon the mature and abiding decisions of the whole Church.[3]

Forty years ago Cardinal Newman made the fol-

[1] A proposal (in effect) to recognize Nonconformist orders as 'valid' in some sense, though irregular. It was sufficiently notorious to be the subject of public sermons.

[2] See *the Conference of Bishops at Lambeth* 1888. *Encyclical letter and reports* pp. 18, 28, 105 ff., esp. p. 110. It was especially the real adherence of our Church to the ancient dogmas and apostolic succession, as having still a living meaning, which could be doubted fifty years ago. "You are so few" (who hold to such things) "that we can count you." See *Loss and Gain* p. 214. In spite of many fears entertained about the 'Pan-Anglican Conference,' it has wrought much good in this way—that the bishops present were in large majority members of unestablished Churches in different lands, and thus the whole basis of discussion was taken off the temporary and accidental basis of an English Establishment.

[3] The Creeds represent decisions. Their whole purpose is to determine. There is no doubt, on the other hand, that, except where the Articles simply express over again the mind of the ancient Church (as in 1.9, 33-34), or pointedly exclude certain mediæval abuses (as in 30 and 32), or Reformation excesses (38, 39), the purpose which governed their wording was to avoid an issue rather than to seek it—to shelve questions, leaving a large tract of open country, rather than to decide them. This characteristic of the Articles is at once their weakness as formulas and their strength as temporary safeguards.

lowing enumeration of the steps which would constitute a 'mortal operation' upon the Anglican Church and destroy its essence or definition : "Take its bishops out of the legislature, tear its formularies from the Statute Book, open its universities to Dissenters, allow its clergy to become laymen again, legalize its private prayer-meetings." Since then three of the contingencies contemplated have actually occurred. Would any one now imagine that the occurrence of the first two would make the operation mortal? Truly God hath done great things for us already, whereof we rejoice.[1]

I shall hope to show in succeeding chapters that Anglicanism is not a mere appeal to precedents—that a real and intelligible groundwork of reason and principle underlies our action and our hopes. For the present I have only two brief remarks to make in order to bring this introductory chapter to a conclusion.

It would be a fatal mistake to suppose that the atti-

---

[1] See Newman *Discourses to mixed Congregations* p. 251. I am sure that so far as there is wilfulness amongst us or within us, we shall all be grateful to Mr. Rivington for making public the private warnings of so great a teacher as Dr. Pusey (*Authority* p. 11). Such warnings we always need. Shall I return good for good, by recalling to Mr. Rivington's notice a *public* warning of Cardinal Newman's of a similar character to his own fellow-clergy? "There are those among us" he wrote (*Letter to the Duke of Norfolk* 1875, p. 4) "as it must be confessed, who for years past have conducted themselves as if no responsibility attached to wild words and overbearing deeds; who have stated truths in the most paradoxical form, and stretched principles till they were close upon snapping; and who at length, having done their best to set the house on fire, leave to others the task of putting out the flame." He goes on to allude to "the chronic extravagances of knots of Catholics."

tude we maintain is that of "Romanism without the Pope." The Roman temper has coloured all her doctrine. It is not only the case that certain doctrines and practices are wholly destitute of authority, except in the Papal system—such doctrines as those of the Treasury of Merits and the Immaculate Conception; but the temper of Rome has coloured further her use of doctrines and practices that are really catholic, not least, perhaps, her doctrine and practice with reference to the sacrament of the Eucharist.[1] The whole logic of Anglicanism forces us, not indeed—God forbid—to

[1] See further p. 176. It will surprise many of us, I think, to read the following statement by Cardinal Newman (1877) of the authoritative Roman doctrine of the Real Presence (*Via Media* ii. p. 220):

"Our Lord is *in loco* in heaven, not (in the same sense) in the sacrament. He is present in the sacrament only in substance, *substantivè*, and substance does not require or imply the occupation of place. But if place is excluded from the idea of the sacramental Presence, therefore division or distance from heaven is excluded also, for distance implies a measurable interval, and such there cannot be except between places. Moreover, if the idea of distance is excluded, therefore is the idea of motion. Our Lord then neither descends from heaven upon our altars, nor moves when carried in procession. The visible species change their position, but He does not move. He is in the holy Eucharist after the manner of a spirit. We do not know how; we have no parallel to the 'how' in our experience. We can only say that He is present, not according to the natural manner of bodies, but *sacramentally*. His Presence is substantial, spirit-wise, sacramental: an absolute mystery, not against reason, however, but against imagination, and must be received by faith."

We cannot but feel as we read this, that this supra-local, spiritual, presence which is not susceptible of change of place—while it agrees very well with the ancient use of the Eucharistic mysteries, agrees very ill with some modern practices, attractive as they are, connected with the Tabernacle and the Monstrance.

ignore the great record of mediæval Christianity, or to cease to venerate the mighty saints of those ages, but to make our appeal on all points behind Roman and mediæval churchmanship to the 'rich depositary' of Scripture and the ancient Church, and make a fresh start from these.

Secondly, it needs to be emphasized that supposing true principles do not force us to accept the present Roman claims, they by that very fact do make the acceptance of them by individuals a grievous betrayal of trust. God has, we must believe, special tasks in store for the Anglican Church, tasks for which the Roman temper and the Roman theology are by their very character and tone disqualified. To some of these we have alluded. It seems likely that it will belong to us, rather than to Rome, to work out the relations of religion to critical knowledge, and to vindicate the true character of inspiration in its relation to historical research. And if these are intellectual problems, there are others in the missionary field and at home of a much more practical sort, over and above the ordinary work of conversion and edification which belongs at all times to all Churches. Now these special tasks of the Church belong to special men. God will raise up, He is raising up, specially gifted men to fulfil them. But we can only do our special tasks through our special men, if we ordinary churchmen and churchwomen are playing our ordinary parts manfully and well. These special vocations, intellectual and spiritual, require a strong background of ordinary church life. It is this thought which ought to enable us all to feel almost

THE ROMAN CHURCH. 23

equally responsible for the general work of the Church —equally bound to merge our individual interests and fears and hopes, even for our own salvation, in the larger interests and fears and hopes of the kingdom of God. Christ, Who said "what is a man profited if he gain the whole world and lose his own soul (life)?" said also, and immediately before it, "whosoever would save his soul (life) shall lose it, and whosoever shall lose his soul (life) for my sake shall find it."[1] Nothing can be so important as to save our soul, our true self, our true life, but we are to look to save it not by selfishly isolating it and sparing it, but by abandoning it to burdens which Christ would lay upon us, and giving it up to His work and His kingdom. The call of Christ to salvation comes not in the way of panic 'amazement' and failing courage, but in the way of endurance, and patience, and forbearance, of greater hope, and firmer ventures of faith and love.

God has a great work to do in reviving the catholic

---

[1] St. Matt. xvi. 25-27. See Revised Version. The word for 'soul' or 'life' is in all cases the same in the Greek and in the Vulgate. I have been led to make the remarks in the text above by Mr. Rivington's intimation (p. 59) that he went to Rome to save his soul from hell. I cannot think that the Bible leads us to suppose that we should save our soul by submitting to the loudest voice, which threatens us with the severest penalties, but rather by following the path of imposed duty with the greatest possible measure of patience and hope, and the venture of faith which holds on to God through all darkness. I should desire a Nonconformist to be brought to the Church by the increasing sense that in proportion as he became unselfish, and threw himself upon the body he belonged to, he became conscious that as a body, as an organization, it did not represent the Divine kingdom, but human self-will.

and free life of the Church of England, and He needs, in different ways, every member of the Church to play a part in it by patience and faith. Who would not rather have stayed in the Church of England forty years ago with Dr. Pusey, patient and faithful, than have left it with others less stable, if more brilliant? The strain, thanks to the faithfulness of him and others like him, has become much less in our day, and the burden less severe. But yet there is much more to be done than God can do in our lifetime, and we meanwhile must see that no cowardice or faintheartedness or impatience of ours hinders its progress.

> ' List, Christian warrior, thou whose heart is fain
> To loose thy mother from her present chain,
> Christ will avenge His Bride—yet ere He save
>   Thy lot shall be the grave.'

CHAPTER II.

THE UNITY OF THE CHURCH.

IT is a question often asked of English churchmen 'In what sense do you believe in *one* Holy Catholic Church? You do not claim that the English Church is of itself and alone the whole Church; you admit the Roman and Eastern branches to be, equally with your own, parts of the Church: that is to say, you admit permanent and apparently radical divisions in the Church in matters of doctrine no less than of government, and yet you say the Church is one. Surely you are here giving words an unreal meaning. Surely the Romanists can call the Church "one" in a much more intelligible sense. What they mean by church unity is plain and tangible. Their Church is one.'

Thus Mr. Rivington has recently said[1]: "I saw that the *plain, obvious* meaning of our Lord's words to St. Peter involved the institution of a visible Head to His visible Church, *besides* the fact that His Church is described as an organized body, and that the talk of a body without a head *in the same order of life* as the rest of the body, is to use words without meaning. An invisible body may have only an invisible head; but a

[1] *Authority* p. 5.

visible body, to be a body at all, must have also a visible head."

In this argument, just quoted, and in the sort of questioning described above, we have specimens of the way in which we are pressed in the English Church to acknowledge that 'logically' the belief in the visible Church leads to Rome; and we make our reply to this solicitation, first, by endeavouring to explain positively the primary sense of church unity, as taught in Scripture and held by the Fathers, so as to show that it covers our position and enables us to give a rational account of it: and then, negatively, by pointing out in what we consider the weakness of the Roman conception of church unity to consist, considered as a *primary* conception.

Primarily, then, the Church is the Spirit-bearing body, and what makes her one in heaven and paradise and earth is not an outward but an inward fact—the indwelling of the Spirit, which brings with it the indwelling of Christ, and makes the Church the great 'Christbearer,' the body of Christ. The principle of unity in any institution or object depends on what it is—on what its essence consists in. The unity of a stone and the unity of a state are different things. The House of Commons is one, and Nature is one; but in different senses. A family again is one, however much brothers may be separated by oceans or kept apart from all intercourse by bitterest feud, because of a community of descent, a common heritage of nature, which runs in the blood and physical constitution, and makes it one. Once more, the Church is one, in a sense to which other unities may supply analogy and illustration, but which is none the less special and unique. She is one because she alone of all societies of men possesses a supernatural indwelling presence and relation to God in Christ. This is a unity which underlies all external separations of place or time, all external divisions and hostilities which result from the marring of the sacred gift by human sin. It is consistent with anything which does not break the channels down which the Church's essence is conveyed from the centre and source of life to all who share it.

Of course this fundamental unity of life is not the only unity. There is a unity of faith, and a unity of love or fellowship also, which we shall have to take into account shortly, but a little examination will show us that this is the principal sense in which Scripture speaks of the Church as one. She is one as the branches are one with the vine[1]: that is, one because the sap of Christ's Life is derived into her, and to be in connection with Christ the source of life is therefore the condition of being in the unity of the Church. Again, Christ prays that His disciples "may be perfected into one" by being taken up through Himself into the fellowship of the life of God.[2] Again when St. Paul speaks of the unity of the Church, he makes it depend—not on subordination to one external government, but—on the

[1] St. John xv. 1-5.
[2] St. John xvii. 22-23 [R.V.]. It should be remarked that Christ did not, strictly, speak of *one fold*, but of *one flock, one shepherd*: 'They shall become one flock.' St. John x. 16 [R.V.]. This is worth notice, though it is sometimes qui e unduly insisted upon.

reception of one food, which is the Life of Christ.[1] Partaking of one Bread we become one Body, 'holding the Head' we share His Life.[2] The unity of the Church is specified to *consist* in 'one body' thus understood, 'one Spirit, one hope, one Lord, one faith, one baptism, one God and Father of all, over all, through all, in all.'[3] It is because the Church possesses this unity that she ought to express it in outward fellowship and peace amongst her members: because we have been "baptized into one body and made to drink of one Spirit," it is incumbent upon us to avoid "schism in the body"[4]: it is because we have the "unity of the Spirit" that we are to endeavour to maintain the "bond of peace."[5] But the unity does not *consist in* the bond of peace: it does not *consist in* outward fellowship, though it ought to result in it.

Metaphors must not be pressed without a very strict regard to the sense in which they are used, and I have been trying to show what is the primary sense in which the one life of the Church is compared in Holy Scripture to the one life of the body and of the vine: it is in the sense that it transmits one life from one source into all its limbs or branches. It is a natural consequence of this way of thinking of Church unity that in Scripture and the early writers it is spoken of as progressive. If the unity of the Church were primarily a unity of outward government it could not *grow*. It would be an external bond once for all imposed. But a unity which is the result of an infused life increases and grows as this new

[1] 1 Cor. x. 14-17.   [2] Eph. iv. 13-16.   [3] Eph. iv. 4-6.
[4] 1 Cor. xii. 13 25.   [5] Eph. iv. 3.

life gains force and absorbs the older elements: so Christ prays that His disciples may be "perfected into one"; and St. Paul speaks of the whole Church growing up "into a perfect man" *i.e.* into a closer and completer unity of life. So in the *Shepherd* of Hermas, sometimes reckoned as Scripture in the early Church, the picture is presented to us of the Church becoming one by gradual purification: "so also shall be the Church of God after it has been purified and the wicked and hypocrites and blasphemers and double-minded have been cast out; after these have been cast out the Church of God shall be one body, one purpose, one mind, one faith, one love" (*Sim.* ix. 18).

The unworthy lives of Christians prevent the Church from manifesting the life of Christ in her, as she is meant to do, and from being the light of the world, but all Christians who believe in a visible Church must admit that there have been times when the Church has been extraordinarily corrupt without losing that intrinsic holiness which belongs to her, because she has the Holy Spirit within her. Again the Church's indolence in Mission work has kept her back from showing to the world that she is truly Catholic and truly adapted to all races. In the same way the divisions in the Church prevent her from bearing the witness she ought to bear to the one life by which she lives; but she no more ceases to be 'one' by outward divisions, than she ceases to be 'holy' by tolerating sin, or 'catholic' because she has so slothfully put up with two-thirds of the world remaining in heathendom. Indeed no one who studies church history can be surprised that a Church which has often looked so utterly unholy, which had even in the fifth century to be described by Salvian as a "sink of vices," should also have grown to look disunited. It would be wonderful if sin had not been as busy to spoil the beauty of the bride of Christ in one way as in the other. The vision of the Church utterly holy, actually catholic, utterly one, is the *vision* of heaven and the *hope* only of earth.

We maintain then that, *primarily*, the unity of the Church is in Scripture a unity of inward life, an invisible fact: it is in this that her essential unity primarily consists. 'But then' it will be said 'you are saying that Church unity is primarily invisible.' We reply that even at this primary stage the unity is external as well as internal. It is quite true that every one who possesses a certain inward gift so far dwells in the unity of the Church. But it is the sacramental principle that the spiritual is imparted (since the Incarnation) through the material. This inward life depends on outward means. Without Baptism, without the "laying on of hands," which gives the gift of the Holy Ghost in His personal indwelling, without the Eucharist, without absolution, we cannot have or retain the inward gift; and those external channels depending, as we all acknowledge they do, on the apostolic ministry, connect the inward life of the Church at once with her outward organization. Every one who has a certain inward gift is in Church unity, but none can, I do not say possess but, make good their claim to possess that gift in its fulness [1] save those who

[1] All baptized persons are in a subordinate sense inside the Church.

THE UNITY OF THE CHURCH. 31

dwell within the unity of the apostolic organization which is the visible Church. It is only through this visible organization that God has covenanted to give us this invisible Life.

"We have from Holy Scripture," wrote Dr. Pusey, "as means and conditions of the unity of the Church, one all-perfect Author, the 'One God and Father of all'; one end to which all tends, the 'one hope of our calling'; 'one Head,' the Head of the Church, our 'one Lord'; 'one Spirit,' giving life to every living member; the same sacraments, 'one baptism,' and 'one bread,' by which we are all ingrafted into or maintained in the one Body of our one Head; one apostolic descent of the bishops and pastors of the flock, coming down from One; 'one' common 'faith,' that which was given once for all with the anathema that we hold no doctrine at variance with it, although an angel from heaven were to preach it. Of these we are receivers only.

"These, if any wilfully reject, they reject Christ. They sever themselves not only from the Body of Christ, but directly from the Head, loosing the band which binds them unto Him. These while Christian bodies retain, they are, so long, like the river which 'went out of Eden to water the garden; and from thence it was parted and became into four heads.' They come from the fountain of blessedness; they flow down to the ocean of the Eternal Love of God; they water the parched land; they cool and refresh the weary and the thirsty in the places which God has appointed for them with the one stream coming down from Him. They are one in their one Original, from which they continually and unchangeably derive their being. They adore God, the Father, Son, and Holy Ghost, with the same new song of the Gospel; they confess Him in the same words of apostolic faith; they offer to Him the same incense of praise, and the same holy offering whereof Malachi foretold, 'from the rising of the sun to the going down of the same,' pleading on earth to the Eternal Father that one sacrifice, as presented in heaven; they receive the same 'bread which came down from heaven to give life to the world.' Unknown in face, in place separate, different in language, opposed, alas! in some things to one another, still before the throne of God they are one holy catholic apostolic Church; each several portion praying for itself and for the rest, united in the prayers and oblations which it offers for all, by the one bread and the one Spirit which dwelleth in all. 'In which mystery' (the holy Eucharist), says St. Cyprian, 'our people are shown to be united, so that, as many grains collected and ground and mingled together make one bread, so in Christ, Who is the heavenly bread, we may know that there is one Body wherewith our whole number is conjoined and united.'"[1]

It will appear plainly enough that this conception of Church unity does not confine it to this world, but includes within it the departed who are, like us, 'in Christ.' It does not allow us to separate off the Church

[1] Dr. Pusey's *Truth and Office of the English Church* pp. 56, 57. A number of patristic passages will be found collected by him p. 45 f. See also in this volume, App. note ii. p. 211.

THE UNITY OF THE CHURCH. 33

Militant and treat it as a separate entity.[1] Further it does not suggest a Head on earth. As the instrument of this unity is the Spirit, as its basis is Christ the Mediator, so the source and centre of it is in the heavens, where the Church's exalted Head lives in eternal majesty human yet glorified. As the bishop is an essential element of the organization of each local Church on earth, so he is the centre of local unity. "There is one flesh of our Lord Jesus Christ," so cried the father Ignatius, who had lived in the apostolic age, "and one cup unto union in the blood: there is one altar as there is one bishop, together with the presbytery and the deacons." But as the Church in each place exists only to bring man into relation to Christ and to the redeemed humanity which Christ is gathering to Himself in the unseen world, so the catholic Church, the society which each local Church represents, has its centre of unity in Christ. "Where the bishop appears, there let the people be; as where is Christ Jesus, there is the catholic Church."[2] Each local Church exists to keep open the connection of earth and heaven: to keep the streams of the water of life flowing. Of course each has a necessary connection with all the others in the witness of truth and in the fellowship of love—we will go on to think of that—but their primary point of union,

[1] F. Richardson *What are the Catholic Claims?* p. 46, complains of me for refusing to treat the Church on earth as a separate unity, complete in itself. He might as well complain of me for refusing to treat of One Person of the Trinity apart from the others.

[2] Ignatius *ad Smyrn.* 8. "The bishop is the centre of each individual Church, as Jesus Christ is the centre of the universal Church."—Lightfoot.

C

the centre to which they all converge, is nothing lower than Christ. The matter cannot be summed up better than in a typical quotation from St. Augustine, which puts this thought in vivid simplicity: "Since the whole Christ is made up of the Head and the body—the Head is our Saviour Himself, who suffered under Pontius Pilate, who now, after He has risen from the dead, sits at the right hand of God: but His body is the Church; not this Church or that, but the Church scattered over all the world; nor that only which exists among men now living, but those belonging to it also who were before us and are to be after us to the end of the world. For the whole Church, made up of all the faithful, because all the faithful are members of Christ, has its Head situate in the heavens which governs this body: though It is separated from their sight, yet It is bound to them by love."[1]

When therefore Roman Catholics speak thus[2]: "There are two intrinsic notes of the Church, *viz.*, one regarding its constitution, *viz.*, that *unity* of government which excludes all schismatical divisions within the body of the Church; and one regarding its life, *viz.*, *holiness* of government"; when they speak of the Church as "'compacted and fitly joined together' with a head appointed by Christ Himself" in virtue of an ordered hierarchy centering in the Pope[3]; when they argue that

[1] St. Aug. *on the Psalms* Ps. lvi. 1.
[2] *The True Basis of Christian Fellowship*, Bishop Meurin, S.J., D.D., p. 32. (It was this book in view of which these papers were first written.)
[3] *The True Basis* etc. p. 70. Cf. Father Gallway's *Lectures on Ritualism* v. p. 175 f. He challenges us to say that "the Head"

two parts of the Church permanently diverging must at last annihilate unity, as a civil war carried to its bitter end makes one nation two—when they argue thus, they are making the unity of the Church primarily an external one, a unity of visible association, the unity which comes of subordination to the same external rule. That this is thoroughly unscriptural has been shown above. That it is inadequate will be seen sufficiently from the consideration that it would exclude the faithful departed from the unity of the Church in its primary sense. For the faithful departed are beyond and above the visible hierarchy on earth. They are in the unity of the Church because that unity is not only of this world—because the Body of Christ has, so to speak, but its lower limbs here on earth. The Church on earth is but the visible portion of a great invisible whole bound all together in the same order of supernatural life.

> "One army of the living GOD,
>   To His command we bow;
> Part of the host have crossed the flood,
>   And part are crossing now."

Mr. Rivington again is making the same mistake when he postulates in the passage quoted above a visible head to the Church on earth. He implies that the unseen Christ and the faithful departed belong to a different "order of life" from the visible body. He would make the Church on earth a complete thing in itself.

whom St. Paul exhorts us "to hold" is the Invisible Head, Christ ! Only 'a Low Churchman or dissenter ought to say so.' Then we may safely be low churchmen or dissenters in company with St. Augustine and the fathers, and the best Roman Commentators.

It is enough to point out how blankly his words contradict what was just quoted from St. Augustine. The Pope becomes, according to this idea, not a *primus inter pares* among bishops, but a quasi-sacramental head, as being the mediator between Christ and His people. Mr. Rivington, indeed, so describes him.[1] I shall have occasion in a later chapter to trace the growth of this quite unprimitive and uncatholic idea. Meanwhile I think enough has been said to show that the true idea of Church unity makes it consist *primarily* in the derivation of the life of the Spirit from Christ, down the channels of His organized society; not in subjection to an external hierarchy centering in the Pope. And this true theory as logically excludes a "sacramental" headship on earth, as the false theory certainly postulates it.

[1] St. Peter (as Head of the Church) is "the sacrament of the administrative power of the one Lord over all" p. 72. "The Papacy is, as it were, the Eucharist of Christ's government in His Church," p. 21. Cf. the *Primary Charge* of the Bishop of Lincoln (Parker), p. 28: "though we would grant the See of Rome her ancient primacy, yet we cannot accept it as it is now offered, transformed into a *quasi*-sacramental Headship."

CHAPTER III.

THE AUTHORITY OF THE CHURCH.

HITHERTO we have been brought to the conclusion that the primary constituent of Church unity is that inward supernatural life, that life of the Spirit, which she derives through sacramental channels from Christ her Head. But besides this unity of life there is a unity of truth, for truth, as well as grace, came by Jesus Christ. There is not only 'one body' but 'one faith.' There is a 'tradition,' 'a form of sound words' committed to the Church in the persons of the Apostles, which is to be the 'mould'[1] of the Christian character so long as the world remains. To the holding of this truth every Christian person or community is bound, and its wilful rejection is what constitutes heresy.

It follows that the Church is not only, through her sacraments, the household of grace: she is also the "pillar and ground of the truth": she has the authority of a divinely authorized teacher, and her legislative enactments in the sphere of truth, no less than of discipline, have a divine sanction. What she binds on

[1] Rom. vi. 17: "The mould of truth into which ye were delivered" (literally).

earth is bound in heaven. And thus Tertullian[1] has *two* questions to ask of any claimants to represent the Church—not only 'have you the apostolic succession?' but also 'do you hold the apostolic truth?' It is then our present task to inquire what this teaching authority of the Church means, in order to be able to answer the question whether the infallibility of the Roman bishop is its logical outcome.

First let it be clear that the Church's function is not to *reveal* truth. The revelation given once for all to the Apostles cannot be either diminished or added to. It is a "faith once for all delivered,"[2] and the New Testament emphasizes the Church's duty as simply that of 'holding fast' and teaching what she has 'received.' The apostle St. Paul claims that his converts should repudiate even him—should treat him as anathema—if he were to teach anything else than what he taught at first.[3] It is thus of the very essence of the Christian revelation that as originally given it is final. Whatever is new to Christian theology in substance, is by that very fact proved not to be of the faith. This is a commonplace of patristic theology, and it is admitted by the modern Roman Church. "First of all" says Dr. Newman "and in as few words as possible, and *ex abundanti cautela*: every Catholic holds that the Christian dogmas were in the Church from the time of the Apostles; that they were ever in their substance what they are now; that they existed before the formulas were publicly adopted, in which as time went on they were defined and re-

---

[1] *de Praescrip.* 32. [2] St. Jude 3 [R.V.].
[3] Gal. i. 8, 9.

THE AUTHORITY OF THE CHURCH. 39

corded."[1] Even the Montanists in ancient time who had a theory of development in discipline, maintained the unchangeableness of the 'rule of faith.' On this subject the 'Reminder' (*Commonitorium*) of Vincent of Lerins has been commonly taken as a summary of patristic teaching, and it is this recognised ancient text-book on the question of Church authority which elaborates the famous formula to express the true creed—that it is what has been held in the Christian Church 'everywhere, always, and by all.' Vincent, then, is never weary of reiterating that novelty is the test of error, antiquity of truth. "To teach anything to catholic Christians[2] besides what they have received, has never been allowed, is nowhere allowed, never will be allowed": "St Paul repeats and reiterates that if any one announces a new dogma, he is to be anathematized."[3] An inquirer who would know the truth when any novel error tries to spread its contagion over the whole Church at once, is "to cling to antiquity, which is quite beyond being seduced by any deception of novelty."[4] He is, as Cyprian says,[5] when the stream of present Church teaching becomes in any way defective, to go to the *source* and repair what

---

[1] *Tracts Theol. and Eccl.* p. 287. We have it on Lord Acton's authority *English Hist. Rev.* Oct. 1890, p. 723, that 'after sixteen years spent in the Church of Rome, Newman was inclined to guard and narrow his theory [of development].' Cf. Keenan's *Controversial Catechism* ed. 1846 p. 117. "Can a General Council frame new matters or articles of faith?" "No; a General Council can only explain what has been already revealed: it belongs to God only to reveal new articles of faith."

[2] He excludes not only what is *contrary to* (*contra*) but what is 'beside' the original deposit (*præter*), cc. 20 and 28.

[3] C. 9.   [4] C. 3.   [5] Ep. 74, 10.

is amiss. Manifestly these writers would not tolerate any depreciation of 'primitiveness' as a test of truth.[1]

It is not then a matter which needs proving, that *novelty* in revelation is equivalent to error, according to the fathers. But this evident proposition leads to an important conclusion. It follows that the authority of the Church is of a more secondary character than is sometimes supposed. She is not a perpetual oracle of divine truth, an open organ of continuous revelation: she is not so much a 'living voice' as a living witness to a once-spoken voice. And it will be observed that whereas the former idea of the Church's function would naturally suggest the probability of a 'central shrine,' where the oracle would be given, a central teaching chair of Christendom—on the other hand the latter idea, that of a witness, suggests the concurrence of manifold traditions. The strength of promulgative authority is centrality; the strength of witness is the consent of independent and distinct voices. Now it is this latter idea of Church authority which is undeniably that of the fathers, always excepting those of the papal school [2] in and after the fifth century. When Tertullian confronts the Gnostics with the *consent* of the different Churches who derived their life and doctrine

---

[1] As Bp. Meurin depreciated it, *True Basis* etc. pp. 30-34. Antiquity is, in Vincent's conception, an *additional* test of truth, besides universality, chap. 27.

[2] I believe, *pace* Mr. Rivington, that this phrase, as I use it, expresses the truth. Papalism began, like the Immaculate Conception, in being the opinion of a school, however much it afterwards won general acceptance in the Churches of the Roman obedience.

THE AUTHORITY OF THE CHURCH. 41

from the Apostles, in a creed the opposite of theirs, when he bids them attend to this consent of Corinth, Ephesus, and Rome, when he asks, in one of his incomparable epigrams whether it is probable that so many Churches of such importance should have hit by an accident of error upon an identical creed; and adds that what is found the same amongst so many, can owe its identity only to its being received by all from a single source,[1] it is obvious that he is viewing the Church's authority as based on the convergence of independent testimonies. He is but taking his idea from Irenaeus,[2] who appeals to the fact that whatever languages the different Churches talk, be they civilized or barbarous, they bear witness to the same creed. This is the principle underlying the authority of general Councils—that their 'generality' secures the elimination of what is merely local or individual and the exaltation of the common heritage. So Vincent of Lerins explains the procedure of the general Council of Ephesus. The authorities of eastern fathers, he tells us, were first recited on the question at issue: then "that not Greece and the East only, but the West and the Latin world as well might be proved to have always held the same sentiments," some authorities were quoted from Rome. After that, "that not the head of the world only but the outlying portions (sides) of it also might give their witness to the judgment," authorities of previous ages were cited from Africa and Milan.[8] Here then is a clear in-

[1] *de Praescr.* 24-36. [2] i. 10. 2, iii. 4. 2.
[8] *Comm.* 30.

telligible principle of consentient witness, eliminating local and individual peculiarities, and it must be allowed to be the principle of the fathers in general and of the Ecumenical Councils. Indeed it is only when we keep this principle in mind that the deference we pay to the decisions of general Councils becomes intelligible. The tone of the actual meeting was sometimes polemical and embittered; that is true at least of the Council of Ephesus, so that it does not present the appearance of a trustworthy spiritual guide, or of a good court of final appeal. But our deference to them becomes quite intelligible when they are considered simply as machinery for registering the agreement of the Churches, and when it is further borne in mind that their authority only became decisive after their verdict had been accepted in the Church at large.[1]

The authority of the Church then is the subordinate authority of a witness to the truth, a guardian, a teacher of it; she has no authority to promulgate or reveal new truth. This is very clearly shown in the difference which St. Athanasius notices between the

---

[1] Three points need to be remembered with reference to these councils: (1) That what was finally authoritative was not the mere council, but the decree of the council when the bishops had separated and their decision had obtained general acceptance.

(2) That the councils simply professed to register and enforce the traditions of the Churches, leaving argument to the theologians.

(3) That our justification in accepting the decisions of the councils lies in the verification of their results taken together. It is most reassuring to find that they represent, not the tyranny of chance majorities, but the gradual working out into a balanced formula of the complex scriptural truth of the Incarnation—guarding it from being overbalanced on one side or the other. The mind of the Spirit is apparent in the result.

formula used by the Fathers of the Council of Nicæa, when settling the Paschal controversy,—a matter of discipline—and when settling the question of faith. 'With reference to Easter' he says,[1] 'such and such things "*were determined*" (ἔδοξε and at such a date), for at that time it was determined that all should obey a certain rule; but with reference to the faith they wrote not "such and such things were determined" but "thus the Catholic Church believes." And they added immediately the statement of their faith, to show that their judgment was not new but apostolic, and that what they wrote was not any discovery of theirs, but was what the apostle taught.'

Thus when the popes began to speak of the 'secret stores' of divine truth (*arcana*) committed to the see of Peter upon which she can draw so as to be the central oracular voice of Christendom, giving replies to the Church in her need,[2] they are beginning to speak in a quite new strain and to give to the Church's authority a new meaning. And it must be observed that this papal idea of a central voice, while it is the natural expression of the idea of promulgative authority, and falls in with the general imperialist tendencies of the Roman Church, is disastrous to the Church's function as a consentient witness. The very centralization of the Roman development removes the security, which the general Councils, truly used, were calculated to

[1] Athan. *de Synodis* 5, quoted by Stanton *Authority in religious belief*, p. 132.
[2] See on the beginning of this tendency in the utterances of Pope Innocent I. in the fifth century, Langen's *Geschichte der römischen Kirche* I. p. 737.

provide, against any local tendency becoming dominant. Thus the Roman centralization is the main cause of what we have already noticed in Roman Catholicism— its one-sidedness. The counter tendencies of other parts of the Church ought to have kept the whole deposit of the faith unnarrowed, by preventing Roman ideas being elevated into catholic dogmas.

According then to the older and really catholic view, the later Church can never know what the early Church did not. She can never have substantially clearer light about the intermediate state, for example, or the relation of the departed to the living, or the 'treasury of merits,' or the position of Mary, than the Church of the second century had. The revelation receives no augmentation, and what for our discipline was left obscure at first, must remain obscure, according to God's providence, till our fragmentary knowledge[1] becomes complete in the Day of Light. It is in fact, as Dr. Salmon remarks, absurd to suppose that the Church's *tradition* can come to convey additional assurance. You cannot have increase of knowledge by tradition. Thus if "the idea of Purgatory had not got beyond a 'perhaps' at the beginning of the fifth century (*i.e.* in St. Augustine's day), we are safe in saying that it was not by tradition that the later Church arrived at certainty on the subject."[2]

Thus we mean broadly by the doctrine which comes on the authority of the Church, the doctrine which

[1] 1 Cor. xiii. 9-12. We know 'in part,' not all: we see a dim reflexion in a mirror.
[2] Salmon *Infallibility* p. 133.

THE AUTHORITY OF THE CHURCH. 45

has been recognised and explicitly taught[1] by the legitimate members of the Christian brotherhood in all ages and all parts of the world: we mean 'historical Christianity.' Is there such a thing? Undoubtedly: and we may add that the whole body of catholic theologians, Roman no less than Anglican, are committed to there being this body of catholic truth, held 'ubique,' that is in all parts, as opposed to any one particular Church: 'semper' always, as opposed to only in recent ages: 'ab omnibus' by all, *i.e.* by the general body of the Church, as Vincent explains, not merely as the private opinion of particular teachers. It will be worth while to quote the summary of the catholic tradition as it is given us for example by Origen in the East, early in the third century, and by Irenaeus in the West, in the latter part of the second.

Tradition, according to Origen, "tells us that there is one God, who created all things out of nothing, who is just and good, the Author of the Old as of the New Testament, the Father of our Lord Jesus Christ: that Jesus Christ was begotten of the Father before every creature, that through Him all things were made, that He is God and Man, born of the Holy Spirit and the Virgin Mary, that He did truly suffer, rise again, and ascend into heaven: that the Holy Ghost is associated in honour and dignity with the Father and the Son, that it is He who inspired the saints both of the Old and of the New Dispensation: that there will be a resurrection of the dead, when the body which is sown

---

[1] *Explicitly*: thus Tertullian specially excludes all idea of a *secret* tradition—*de Praescr.* 25-27.

in corruption will be raised in incorruption, and that in the world to come the souls of men will inherit eternal life or suffer eternal punishment according to their works: that every reasonable soul is a free agent, plotted against by evil spirits, comforted by good angels, but in no way constrained: that the Scriptures were written by the agency of the Spirit of God, that they have two senses, the plain and the hidden; whereof the latter can be known only to those to whom is given the grace of the Holy Spirit in the word of wisdom and knowledge."[1] This he "gives as 'the teaching of the Church' transmitted in orderly succession from the apostles, and remaining in the Churches to the present day," as the authoritative standard of belief.

Now let us listen to Irenaeus: "The true knowledge" (so he calls the Christian religion) "is the doctrine of the Apostles, and the ancient system of the Church in all the world: and the character of the body of Christ, according to the successions of the bishops, to whom they (the Apostles) delivered the Church in each separate place: the complete use (moreover) of the Scriptures which has come down to our time, preserved without corruption, receiving neither addition nor loss; its public reading without falsification; legitimate and careful exposition according to the Scriptures, without peril and without blasphemy: and the pre-eminent gift of love." Again, "The way of those who belong to the Church is encompassing the whole world, because it holds the tradition firm from

[1] See Dr. Bigg's *Bampton Lectures* p. 152. This 'rule of faith' is abbreviated from the Preface to the *De Principiis*.

the Apostles, and enables us to see that the faith of all is one and the same, while all accept one and the same God the Father, and believe the same dispensation of the Incarnation of the Son of God, and acknowledge the same gift of the Spirit, and meditate the same precepts, and preserve the same form of that ordination which belongs to the Church, and expect the same coming of the Lord, and await the same salvation of the whole man, both soul and body."[1]

Origen and Irenaeus are not speaking exhaustively, and there can be no reasonable doubt that as a matter of historical evidence, the Church always believed not only the doctrines of the Trinity and the Incarnation, of the Atonement won in Christ, of the inspiration of Scripture, of resurrection and judgment, of the visible Church, and of the apostolic ministry; but also the doctrine of the sacraments as channels of grace, and of the Eucharist as a sacrifice.[2]

Of this sort then is the historic creed of Christendom, which has been held and publicly taught as Christianity over the whole area of the Church. The denial of any of these elements of belief has always brought a man under suspicion and in the last resort constituted him a formal heretic or schismatic. The Church had indeed immense difficulty in formulating her theology—for example, in making out of human language a formula to guard the truth of the Trinity. There is therefore a certain ambiguity of *language* on some points in the

[1] See Irenaeus, iv. 33. 8, v. 20. 1.
[2] On the three last points I may refer to *The Church and the Ministry* see esp. p. 213: and cap. vii. p. 78 n.[1], p. 226 n.[1].

early theology, though this fact easily admits of being exaggerated. But there is in substance an outspoken expression of this body of truth, in the strictest sense catholic, in the Church. It does not require any very profound or wide reading to discover that the early Church did believe in the sacraments, though the belief was not formulated into dogmas, and did not believe in a treasury of merits which the pope could dispense in indulgences, or an immaculate conception of the blessed Virgin, or an infallibility of the pope. But of this somewhat more hereafter.

And how does this 'general consent' express itself? Let Vincent of Lerins answer. Let us hear what he bids the perplexed inquirer do, amid the manifold heresies of the fifth century, to ascertain the true faith. First he is to seek the authority of general Councils, where such have been held. Their decrees rank first, as authorized and final interpreters of Scripture. But if a new question arises on which no such Council has spoken, then he is to collect the sentiments of the ancients; of those, that is, who remained in the communion of the Church, masters of repute. And here care is to be taken to adhere to no individual opinion of however great a Christian, but to that teaching only in which they are found to agree.[1] This advice is given to ordinary individual Christians again and again.

And now what is the Roman objection to the idea of authority which has just been explained? It may be said to be threefold.

(1) It will be said[2]: "It is not easy then to find out

[1] cc. 28, 29. [2] As by Mr. Rivington p. 29.

what is catholic on your showing. We have contradictory statements made about what the fathers teach. How are we—not professed theologians or even students—to find out the 'rule of faith'? The Roman idea of Church authority gives a simpler remedy for our difficulties. *Theirs* is a rule of faith of easy access."

To this the answer is that with us too the *proximate* rule of faith is of easy access. The individual Churchman begins by submitting himself to be moulded by the rule of faith which he receives. The proximate authority for each of us consists of the personal teachers to whom by God's providence we are subject, though, from the first, side by side with the personal teachers, and controlling them, are the written formulas of the Church, which she propounds to guide the faith and practice of all her members,—the creed and the catechism, the offices and ceremonies. Thus the personal teachers and the formulas, taken together, constitute the proximate rule of faith. In the assimilation of this each individual finds his primary responsibility. For the apprehension of it there is no need of research. 'The word is very nigh thee.' Nor, if it is defective or superstitious, will God's requirement of truth extend beyond each man's opportunities.

But this proximate rule of faith is not the ultimate authority. It is this ultimate rule of authority—the 'remoter rule'—with which we have been occupied in this chapter. So far as this again is based on Scripture, all Christians have easy access to it, but with that we are not yet concerned. This remoter rule of faith involves, as we have now seen, a comparison of records, a searching into the past traditions of the Church. Such research is only possible, comparatively, for a few, and only a few are capable of undertaking it. But the few act for the many. The fact that competent persons are constantly engaged in this verifying process of comparison and research guarantees that the current Church teaching is being kept pure from accretion. No doubt, however, this verifying process involves difficulty, and it is one in which to a certain extent all are concerned. What shall we say in regard to the charge that it is difficult?

We reply that there is no reason why it should not be difficult. The fathers do not seem to shrink from recommending, even to ordinary inquirers, a difficult way of arriving at the truth. They do not speak as men who have any 'short and easy' method to recommend,[1] and we would add that in the early centuries such short and easy method was, it would appear,

[1] See Mahan's *Exercise of Faith* (J. G. Palmer, London, 1877) p. 68. "Let us take such a case, for example, as that so graphically described by St. Chrysostom; a case which might have occurred at any time during the first six centuries, and which may occur every day now. A heathen comes forward desiring to be a Christian. He consults so eminent and enlightened a bishop as St. Chrysostom. He says, 'I desire to be a Christian, but to *whom* shall I attach myself? In the contention, and division, and confusion among you all, which dogma shall I take? Which shall I prefer? Since all of you profess to hold the truth, which shall I believe? I know nothing at all of Scriptures; and they who profess to know, produce the same proofs for their respective tenets.' To this Chrysostom replies, 'I am glad that all parties agree thus far; for if we referred you only to reason, you might be justly at a loss; but if we send you to the Scriptures, and they are simple and true, your decision is easy: for *whoever accords with them, he is a Christian; but whoever is at variance with them is very far from it.*' But the man rejoins, 'I have searched the Scriptures, and find that they teach

more 'imperatively needed' than it has ever been since. There was never, perhaps, a time of confusion in the Christian Church equal to the second century. Christianity seemed to the philosopher outside a chaos of dissentient sects, "agreeing in nothing but the name."[1] The various forms of Gnosticism were so seductive that Tertullian witnessed in his day the spectacle of "one and another—the most faithful, the wisest, the most experienced in the Church, going over to the wrong side."[2] The points under discussion were the most fundamental conceivable, the questions of the creation of the world, the unity of God, and the reality of the Incarnation. If ever a clear rule of faith, a papal voice, a centre to Christendom was needed, it was then. But not only had the Church at that time to struggle through her difficulties without an infallible teacher, she had not even yet formulated her creeds or settled her canon. Once more, the years of the Arian contro-

one thing, and you another. What, then, am I to do? Must I make myself a teacher, when I know nothing of the matters at issue, and desire merely to be a learner?'

"Now here is the point at which, if anywhere, the infallible guide is needed. This is the case that demands the simple explicit answer to the question, 'Whom and what shall I believe?' And if Chrysostom and other Church teachers of the first 'six centuries could give *no such single test of truth,* and no such absolute direction as the case demanded, it proves either that they knew no such simple direction; or else, if they knew it, that they handled the word of God deceitfully, and perplexed the simple souls whom it was their business to guide. In this particular instance, St. Chrysostom, after asking the man whether he had not *a mind* and *judgment of his own,* proceeds to give him such marks of the true Church as he could, and leaves him to make his way clear through the mazes of this complex guidance." (St. Chrysostom *Homilies on the Acts,* xxxiii. in *Library of Fathers* part ii. pp. 462-7.)

[1] Origen *c. Cels.* iii. 12.   [2] *de Praescr.* 3.

versy[1] were years of deepest distress. Again a papal voice of authority was sorely needed, if ever. But in the moment of uttermost strain and profoundest peril, the pope did something very different from giving a clear voice for the guidance of Christians. He repudiated Athanasius the great upholder of the truth, and left him alone 'against the world.'[2] The fact is, the argument from the supposed needs of man to the existence of an infallible teaching chair breaks down historically from the fact that, in the hours of greatest need in the Church, there was no remedy such as it is now suggested that man imperatively requires—there was no quick method of finding out the truth. And indeed is not this difficulty, this requirement of patience, in finding out the truth, part of the probation of faith? It is just what is suited to our time of discipline. At any rate we have no right to claim of God the removal of certain difficulties. We must take His revelation under the conditions on which He gives it, and endure what the fathers endured. We make a great mistake about the essence of faith if we imagine that faith is merely the surrendering of our reason and the passive acceptance of an unmistakable voice of external authority. Faith, in the Bible, is opposed not to *reason*, but to *sight*. It was not Christ's will to reveal Himself beyond all possibility of doubt. He did not utter a dogma about Himself and bid men bow down to it. The faith which could accept Him had to see through a veil. When men complained that He kept their souls in uncertainty, when they importunately asked to be 'told plainly,'[3] He made

---

[1] See App. note iii. p. 212. [2] See Chapter **VI**. [3] St. John x. 24.

no response to their complaint, except to attribute their unbelief to their not being 'His sheep.' Faith is an inner sense which faithfully and perseveringly apprehends God in spite of difficulties and through the veil. The faith which was required to believe in Christ in spite of ambiguities is the same faith which is required to believe in the Church. And practically a prayerful and patient Christian *can* find out the mind of the Church with quite sufficient security. The current teaching of the Church about what is contained in the Creeds, and about the Sacraments and Ministry has almost always been sufficiently explicit and clear for simple minds, and has afforded a basis of security in the strength of which it is good for most of us to feel a certain amount of hesitation and to experience the necessity of feeling our way.

(2) But it is objected further: 'an authority which leaves you partly dependent on your own reason and judgment is no authority at all. To accept authority is the opposite of what you call "feeling one's own way."' Thus Father Richardson defines the authority of the Church as 'the absolute, peremptory power from which there is no appeal, exercised by a living existing voice, commanding the assent of the intellect in God's name, and speaking as God's instrument.'[1] To this it is only necessary here to give a brief answer. God deals with us as with sons, not as with slaves. He makes us partakers of His counsels, intelligent co-operators with Him. Our attitude towards Him is not 'abject.'[2] It

[1] *What are the Catholic Claims?* p. 51.
[2] As Mr. Ward described it: see *W. G. Ward and the Oxford Movement*, by Wilfrid Ward (Macmillan, 1889) p. 216, but *cf.* St. John xv. 15.

is only to put this in other words to say that authority is not the same thing as absolutism, which is only an exaggerated and perverted form of it. True authority does not issue edicts to suppress men's personal judgment or render its action unnecessary, but it is like the authority of a parent, which invigorates and encourages, even while it restrains and guides the growth of our own individuality. I do not wish to enlarge on this idea here, but I am sure I shall do well to repeat a question asked long ago on this subject. "Is a limited, conditional government in the State such a wise, excellent, and glorious constitution? And is the same authority in the Church such absurdity, nonsense, and nothing at all, as to any actual power? If there be such a thing as obedience upon rational motives, there must be such a thing as authority that is not absolute, or that does not require a blind, implicit obedience. Indeed, rational creatures can obey no other authority; they must have reasons for what they do. And yet because the Church claims only this rational obedience, your Lordship explodes such authority as none at all."[1] I must protest that the authority of the Church is, as we Anglicans understand it, a most real guidance of our spirit and intellect, to which, by God's mercy, we love to submit ourselves. Submission to that authority is in the first instance the putting ourselves to school under the Church's primary teaching. Beyond this, as we grow in knowledge, it is the merging of our mere individualism in the whole historic life of the great

[1] Law's *First Letter to the Bishop of Bangor* in his *Works* [ed. 1762] i. pp. 30, 31.

Christian brotherhood; it is making ourselves at one with the one religion in its most permanent and least merely local form. It is surrendering our individuality only to empty it of its narrowness. One with the Christianity of history, the Christianity of creeds and councils, we enter into the heritage of her dogmas and of something as great as her greatest dogmas, the whole joy of her sacraments, the security of her ministry, the communion of her saints, the fellowship of her Spirit. We can read her great fathers and find ourselves one with them in all important matters of faith [1] over the lapse of ages. The hearts of the fathers are seen to be turned towards their children. We believe in the Holy Catholic Church.

(3) 'But,' it is said—and it is the last objection I will consider—'on your own showing the final court of appeal is no longer open to you. You can no longer summon a general council, or what you would acknowledge as such.' To this our answer is partly that we admit our grievous loss, but it is not our fault. With what infinite joy would we hail its possibility! But there is a further answer. A general council is not a necessity. It was impossible from one set of causes for the first three hundred years, but all through that period men like Irenaeus and Tertullian were not prevented from arriving at the mind of the Church by the comparison of traditions. "The judgment of the Church *diffusive*" says Mr. Wilberforce "is no less binding than that of the Church *collective*."[2] The consent of the Church as

---

[1] Not of criticism or of science, however, which are progressive in a sense in which Revelation is not.
[2] *Principles of Church Authority* p. 77.

it was discoverable before general councils were possible from one set of reasons, so is still discoverable by us since they have become impossible from another. Beyond this we must content ourselves with councils less than ecumenical, though resting on their basis, and it is quite possible that it was not intended in God's providence that the formulation of ecumenical dogmas should go beyond defining the basis of the Christian faith and life, as it is given in the Creeds. The imposition of a dogma as a condition of communion is a necessary evil which should be kept within the smallest limits possible in view of the Church's safety.: and a Church shows her life not by creating new dogmas but by living on the old faith and 'commending it to every man's conscience' by rendering it intelligible in view of new needs to new generations of men.

It is necessary to lay down briefly, before we conclude, the sense in which we can accept of 'development' in Christian truth.[1] In such sense as makes it concerned only with the *statement* of truth, we accept and indorse the idea. In this sense Vincent of Lerins makes it the Church's duty to develop truth. His words are exact and well worth quoting[2]: "The Church of Christ, the anxious and careful guardian of the truths committed to her, never changes anything in them, diminishes nothing, adds nothing, neither cuts off what is needful, nor appends what is superfluous: does not lose what is her

[1] See also App., note i. p. 203.
[2] *Common.* c. 23. The whole chapter should be read. The earlier part speaks of the growth of 'religion' as a whole. It grows as a child grows to manhood. Each limb increases in size, but no new limb is added, or old one removed. Then it passes to the development of the *doctrine* of the Church.

own, nor incorporate what is not, but devotes all her pains to this one task—by dealing faithfully and wisely with old truths, to give perfection and finish to whatever was of old left shapeless and inchoate; to consolidate and establish what has been already expressed and developed; to preserve what has been already established and defined.... When she was roused by the novelties of heretics, the catholic Church, by the decrees of Councils, has ever effected this and nothing more—that she should consign to posterity in the security of a formal document, what she had received from her ancestors by mere tradition, summarizing great matters in a few words, and generally, with a view to greater clearness, stamping with the speciality of a new term an article of the faith which was not new."

In reference then to the Church's *terminology* we accept the principle of development in the rule of faith, but no further.[1] In such sense as can make it cover the extension of the substance of the faith, so as to include an article such as the Immaculate Conception,

[1] That is, as touches the faith. In discipline there is confessedly development and in the use of the sacraments, provided there is no alteration in doctrine. Thus the practice of reserving confirmation to a later age, and making it the occasion for a renewal of vows, or again the practice of encouraging those who are not at the time communicants to assist at the Eucharist, are developments in practice and discipline, which involve no development in doctrine. I think the maximum of development which is to be found in the early Church is that involved in the recognition of ordinations administered by heretics. I have briefly traced the history of this in *The Church and the Ministry* pp. 187-196. But in any case the development did not touch *the faith of individuals*: all that was in question was how the official Church was to act in the light of her faith about orders, in view of a difficulty where antagonistic truths seemed to collide.

—an idea utterly outside the horizon of a Chrysostom or an Augustine—in such sense we repudiate it. Indeed in her official documents the Roman Church herself prefers to take the line which puts her most in conflict with history, and setting aside the larger idea of development, proclaims her modern dogma of the Infallibility as belonging to the "tradition received from the beginning of the Christian faith."

On the other hand some modern Roman theologians, of whom the ablest is Cardinal Franzelin, convinced apparently of the impossibility of showing that the modern Roman dogmas were recognized, in substantial reality at least, if not in set terms, in the early Church, repudiate the Vincentian canon, in its only intelligible sense, or, in other words, in the sense of its author. "The rule of Vincent" says Cardinal Franzelin "is true in its positive sense (*i.e.* any doctrines which have been openly taught and believed 'ubique, semper, ab omnibus,' are necessarily of faith), but it cannot be admitted in a negative or exclusive sense." "It is contrary to the whole economy of the faith" to say that "only those things which have been explicitly believed from the first are contained in the deposit of the faith." "It is enough to have shown a consent of faith prevailing in the Church at any time in the apostolic succession" *e.g.* the present time "in order to vindicate the divine revelation and apostolic tradition of any head of doctrine."[1] It is only necessary to point out that this is not to interpret Vincent, but to repudiate him. Vincent un-

---

[1] Franzelin *De Divina Traditione et Scriptura* ed. 3. Rome 1882. Thesis ix. Coroll. 1. p. 87. Thesis xii. Schol. i. Princip. ii. Coroll. 4 p. 121. Thesis xxiv. p. 221.

doubtedly meant to make his rule an *exclusive test*. He excludes not only what is contrary to (contra), but also what is 'beside' (praeter) the original deposit.[1] Further, he makes antiquity an additional test of truth, besides present consent.[2] In the sense then that would make the obligatory Christian doctrine or common rule of faith, a germ developing in content and extent, we exclude development.

There is indeed another sense in which the whole life of the Church is constantly developing, as she expands to embrace new material, and brings forth out of her treasury, like a wise householder, things new and old. But such developments to cover new needs can never antiquate the rule of faith. That is adequate for all races, all ages, all contingencies, and as it is with it alone that we are at present concerned, so we protest that for our 'rule of faith' we own with the ancient Church nothing narrower than what was held and taught in all parts of the world, and from the first, and as the common tradition of the Church at large; and we are sure that any advantages which may be gained by narrowing its basis are more than compensated for by the infinite evils which accrue from limiting the tradition of truth within the channel of a single, however powerful, Church.

[1] Capp. 20, 28.   [2] Capp. 3, 9, 27.

CHAPTER IV.

THE BIBLE IN THE CHURCH.

IN this discussion it may be assumed as a point outside controversy that the Bible does not stand alone as the rule of faith, any one being permitted to interpret it according to his or her isolated judgment.[1] The Church, in fact, existed before the books of the New Testament were written; they were written for those who were already members of the Church and had received her primary instruction;[2] they continually refer back to that primary instruction and pre-suppose it;[3] the Church

[1] It is important to observe, however, that most of the books of the New Testament, considered merely as historical documents, will stand alone without needing any witness of the Church, beyond merely such historical witness as church writings give to their existence and diffusion. Thus we must trust to purely critical grounds for justifying the historical character of the Gospel history and the Acts of the Apostles. Mere historical evidence has justified the belief that St. John wrote the fourth Gospel, and that St. Paul wrote the epistles ascribed to him. Once more historical evidence requires us to believe that the anonymous Epistle to the Hebrews was written by an "apostolic man" before the destruction of Jerusalem. But these books of the New Testament, thus historically certified, bear witness to the Church, and refuse to be detached from her.

[2] St. Luke i. 4; 1 Cor. i. 5, xi. 2, 23, xvi. 5; Heb. v. 12; 2 Peter i. 12; Jude 3; 1 John ii. 20.

[3] See reff. in last note and 1 Timothy iii. 15. The Church is the basis upon which the human witness to the revealed truth ultimately rests.

gradually collected them into a canon and drew the line between the Epistle to the Hebrews in which she recognised primary or apostolic authority, and the Epistle of Clement or the *Shepherd* of Hermas in which she did not; and finally in history the Bible came out into the world simply as the sacred books of a certain society, the Church, accessible to her members and belonging to her alone. All this being so, it may be taken for granted that the Bible does not stand alone as giving the Christian rule of faith, but the Bible interpreted by the Church. The Spirit in the society interprets the Spirit in the books.

Thus we may even assume, at starting, the extreme position of Tertullian when he refuses (rhetorically, not in fact) even to argue the meaning of Scripture with people who do not belong to the historical Christian Church.[1] "Our appeal (in argument with persons outside the Church) must not be made to the Scriptures, nor must controversy be admitted under circumstances where victory will be either impossible or uncertain or not certain enough. For even if a comparison of Scripture should not turn out in such a way as to put the disputants on a level, still the logical order required another question, as yet the only question, to be first propounded,—To whom does the faith itself belong? Whose are the Scriptures? From whom, and through whom, and where, and to whom has been handed down that discipline by which men become Christians? For wherever it shall appear that the reality of the Christian discipline and faith are to be found, there will be also

[1] *de Praescr.* 19.

the reality of the Scriptures and of the interpretations and of all Christian traditions."

Assuming this general position as lying behind the divergence of the Anglican and Roman branches of the Church, a further question arises as to the relation in which the authority of the Church tradition stands to the authority of Scripture. The view of the Anglican Church is clear. Scripture is the final court of appeal in matters of faith, "so that whatsoever is not read therein, nor may be proved thereby, is not to be required of any man that it should be believed as an article of the faith, or be thought requisite or necessary to salvation." The Church finds her sphere of authority only in interpreting and teaching the faith contained in Scripture. A canon of the convocation which imposed on the clergy subscription to the Articles, directs preachers " to be careful that they never teach aught in a sermon, to be religiously held and believed by the people, except what is agreeable to the doctrine of the Old and New Testaments, and what the catholic Fathers and ancient bishops have collected from that same doctrine." The Bible is the ultimate record of the faith: the Church is the interpreter. The Church is the primary teacher of the truth to her children but she sends them to the Scriptures to verify it for themselves.

With this position of the Church the Romanist writers and authorities are not in the main satisfied. The Council of Trent[1] declares that "the truth" of the Christian Revelation "is contained in the written books *and* in the unwritten traditions" and that the Council

---

[1] Sess. iv.

"receives and venerates *with an equal feeling of piety and reverence all the books of the Old and New Testament . . . and also the traditions relating as well to faith as to morals*, as having, either from the word of Christ Himself or the dictation of the Holy Ghost, been preserved by continuous succession in the catholic Church." The teaching of the Roman Church thus makes tradition an authority independent of holy Scripture, so that Scripture is only the *chief source*[1] of catholic truth, but an article of the faith may rest on church teaching alone, as a sufficient basis in itself. This theoretical departure from what we propose to show to have been the primitive conception of the authority of Church tradition, has resulted in a corresponding departure from primitive practice. The early Church, believing the Bible to be the guide of individual Christians in faith and conduct, would have all her members well versed in its contents. They could safely read the Scriptures for themselves and be earnestly exhorted to do so, if only the Church's teaching had first given them the right point of view for their study. Thus guided by the mind of the Church, they were bidden to see for themselves whether the whole teaching of the Church was not to be found in

[1] Cornely *Hist. et Crit. Introd. in V. T. Compendium* Paris 1889 p. 1, speaks thus of the Holy Scriptures: "Ex illis utpote praecipuo revelationis fonte, ecclesia dogmata sua hausit, hauritque." It has been questioned whether the Roman Church is dogmatically committed to the view of tradition which makes it an independent source of truth, parallel to Scripture. The words of the Council of Trent have been explained in a more moderate sense, and there are some Roman theologians on this side. But the practice of the Roman Church and her common teaching is as indicated above. See on the subject Palmer *On the Church* ii. 10-18.

Scripture. Thus the familiarity of the whole body of the people with the original record would serve to maintain a scriptural tone and to keep the Church's current teaching and system from deterioration. The Roman Church, on the other hand, practically makes ordinary Christians only come in contact with the Bible at second-hand. The Church teaches and the laity receive. They are not encouraged to drink for themselves at the fountain-head of Scripture.[1] It is obvious enough what danger this must involve of the Church system becoming autocratic, arbitrary, external, when the check is removed which a generally diffused knowledge of Scripture, always antagonistic to such tendencies, is alone calculated to supply. It is also obvious what audacity is involved in this withdrawal of Scripture into the background, if our Lord's intention was that Scripture should be the constant practical guide of individual souls. We proceed, without further discussion, to illustrate by some quotations the relation in which the Fathers conceived the Church to stand towards the Bible, and the urgency with which they pressed on the laity the free study of Scripture.

Let us listen first to Vincent of Lerins, who holds, as we saw in our last discussion, so remarkable a position in relation to the theory of Church authority.

"Often" he says,[2] "have I inquired with great care

---

[1] This is admitted by Cardinal Manning in a passage quoted in chap. I, and I do not suppose it will be denied. I am of course aware that Lacordaire and others recommended the freer use of Scripture, but they represented tendencies other than Ultramontane, and the fact at least is as Cardinal Manning states.

[2] *Common.* c. ii.

THE BIBLE IN THE CHURCH. 65

and much earnestness, of very many men eminent for holiness and doctrine, how I might, by some certain, and, as it were, general and regular way, discern the truth of the catholic faith from the falsehood of heretical pravity: and have always received, from all of them, an answer of this sort: that I, or any other person, wishing to detect the frauds of heretics as they rise, and avoid their snares, so as to keep himself in a sound faith whole and sound, must, with the help of the Lord, fortify his faith in a twofold manner; first, namely, by the authority of the law of God; and then, in the next place, by the tradition of the catholic Church.

"Here, perhaps, some one will ask, What need is there—seeing that the canon of the Scriptures is perfect, and in itself suffices to the full, and more, for all demands —that the authority of the ecclesiastical interpretation should be joined to it? Because the holy Scripture, for its very depth, is not taken of all in one and the same sense; but its expressions are interpreted diversely, by one man in one way, by another in another, so that it seems as if almost as many opinions may be gathered out of it as there are men. . . . . . It is, therefore, very necessary, on account of the vagaries of errors so manifold, that the line of interpretation of the prophetical and apostolical writings be drawn by the rule of the ecclesiastical and catholic sense."

Again, at the end of his little treatise [1] he sums up thus:—

"We said in the premises, that this always hath

---
[1] *Common.* c. xxix.

been, and even at this day is, the custom of Catholics, to try and examine the true faith, by these two methods. First, by the authority of the divine canon: secondly, by the tradition of the catholic Church; not because the canonical Scripture is not of itself sufficient for all things, but because very many expounding GOD's word at their own pleasure, conceive hereby divers opinions and errors. And for that cause, it is necessary that the interpretation of the heavenly Scripture be directed according to the one only rule of the Church's understanding: only, be it observed, especially in those questions upon which the foundations of the whole catholic doctrine depend."

Now I cite an eastern and earlier authority, Origen [1]: "In the two testaments every word that pertaineth unto God may be sought and discussed, and out of them all knowledge of things may be understood. And if anything remains which Holy Scripture does not determine, no other third scripture ought to be received to authorize any knowledge, but we must 'commit to the fire' what remains, that is, reserve it unto God. For God did not will us to know all in the present life, as the apostle specially says *we know in part*. . . . Do not let us, then, with the presumption of rashness, assume to ourselves the knowledge of everything, lest the same apostle rebuke us as *knowing neither what they speak nor of what they affirm.*" How, on the other hand, Origen insisted on ecclesiastical tradition as guiding our search into Scripture, appeared in the citation from him in the last

[1] *Hom. in Lev.* v. 9 tom. ii. p. 212.

chapter. I will only quote one other authority in this matter—the authority of the great name of St. Athanasius.[1] There is no father more scriptural than St. Athanasius in his method of argument. He insists strongly on the sufficiency of Holy Scriptures "in which alone is the instruction of religion announced—to which let no man add, from which let no man detract— which are sufficient in themselves for the enunciation of truth," but he also insists that a 'point of view' is necessary in reading and interpreting Scripture, and this point of view is the 'Church's mind.' Where the meaning of Scripture is doubtful in itself, it is enough that it 'admits' an interpretation in accordance with the Faith.

[1] It would however be easy to multiply references, see esp. Palmer *On the Church* ii. pp. 10 ff. Harold Browne *Thirty-Nine Articles* on Art. vi. The reference above is to Athanasius *adv. Gentes* init. and *Fragm. Fest. Ep.* xxxix. St. Basil has a passage *de Spir. Sanct.* xxvii. § 66, which, when divorced from its context, appears to countenance the Roman view, and to give 'the unwritten tradition' 'the same force' as Holy Scripture in what the Church holds and declares. But in illustrating what he means, he speaks under the head of tradition only of church practices and rules of discipline (turning to the east, formulas of consecration, ceremonies of baptism, etc.). Such are the 'dogmata' or 'ordinances' which he assigns to tradition. On the other hand, when writing *De Fide* c. 1, he makes the Scripture the sole source of the faith. "It is a manifest falling from the faith, and an argument of arrogancy, either to reject any point of these things that are written, or to bring in any of these things that are not written." The fathers in general draw a distinction between the authority of Scripture for doctrine and the authority of unwritten tradition for practice. Cf. Tertul. *De corona* 3, 4. St. Chrysostom on 2 Thess. ii. 15, and Epiphanius *Haer.* lxi. 6, should be interpreted in accordance with this principle. Cf. Salmon *Infallibility* pp. 142-3, and Mason *Conditions of Our Lord's Earthly Life* (Longmans, 1896) pp. 6 f., who adds: "I do not know one article of belief which is asserted by the Fathers to be derived from tradition outside of the cause of Scripture."

That is to say, the Church is neither more nor less than the authorized interpreter of Scripture.

The following references will indicate how free the Fathers are in urging on Christians the direct study of Scripture. "Do not" St. Cyril of Jerusalem says,[1] speaking even to catechumens, "do not believe me simply, *unless you receive the proof of what I say from Holy Scripture.*" And, exhorting his hearers not to study the apocryphal books, he bids them give zealous attention to the canonical Scriptures. Again, in his next lecture,[2] he bids them "keep that faith only which the Church is now giving to you and which is certificated out of the whole of Scripture." Again, "'Tis from ignorance of Scripture," says Chrysostom, in the beginning of his *Homilies on the Romans*,[3] "that all our evils arise; hence the plague of so many heresies, hence our careless lives, our fruitless labours. . . . They err who look not to the bright rays of the divine Scriptures, because they walk in darkness."[4] When he is preaching his running commentaries on the New Testament, he recommends his hearers to read the passage on which he is preaching before they come to Church, and afterwards to keep quiet at home and study it with their families. "The source of error," says Pope Leo in his famous tome,[5] "is that when men are hindered by some obscurity in knowing the truth, they run not to prophets, or apostles, or evangelists, but to themselves"; they will not "labour in the broad field of Holy Scripture."

[1] A.D. 348 *Catech.* iv. 17, 33.
[2] A.D. 348 *Catech.* v. 12.
[3] Tom. ix. p. 426.
[4] *Hom. in Matt.* i. v. tom. vii. pp. 13, 72.
[5] *Ep.* xxviii. 1.

These few examples must suffice. But such quotations might be multiplied indefinitely. They illustrate two facts: the theory of the fathers that Scripture is the sole *source* of revealed truth—and their practice, based on this theory, of enjoining on all Christians its free study.[1]

The patristic conception of the rule of faith finds it, as we have seen, (*a*) in the Bible, (*b*) in the witness of the general Church interpreting the Bible. Let us briefly indicate to what results the application of this test will lead us. It will lead us to accept first of all those central doctrines of the faith, the Incarnation, and the Trinity, which the Church has formulated in definite dogmas, and which we can, guided by the Church, find clearly enough for ourselves in Scripture—and also the doctrines of the Inspiration of Scripture and of the Atonement, which Scripture declares and which the Church has always believed and inculcated, though there is a remarkable absence of definite dogmas to make an exact claim on our belief on these subjects. Next we shall accept all that body of truth, which is the 'extension of the Incarnation'—the doctrines of Baptismal Regeneration, of the gift of the Spirit in Confirmation, of the Eucharistic Presence and Sacrifice, of the Ministry with its authority in Absolution, and of the visible Church. Two of these doctrines are more or less explicitly stated in the creeds. The rest are parts of the universal Church's teaching and are also contained, as we can verify for ourselves, in the

[1] That it was practicable for Christians of the Roman Empire to possess and read for themselves the books of Scripture, see App. note iv. p. 213.

language of Scripture.¹ These too we shall receive as
'of faith,' even though the absence of definite dogma
must make us careful in imputing *heresy* to those
whose teaching on the subject is not explicit.² When a
doctrine is plainly stated in Scripture, like the doctrine
of eternal punishment, or of man's free-will on the one
hand, and fallen nature on the other, then the general
consent of the Church will confirm us in maintaining
them, and we shall not be restrained from doing so by
the aberrations of individual teachers.³ Where a doctrine
has been commonly held by churchmen, like the actual
sinlessness of the blessed Virgin, but cannot either plead
quite universal consent nor the authority of Scripture,
it will rank rather as a pious opinion than as an article
of faith. Where an opinion has been held commonly in
Christendom for a while and then abandoned, without
being explicitly condemned, as out of harmony with
Scripture and reason, like the notion of Christ's offering
His death as ransom to the devil, then we shall not
scruple to reject what lacks *permanent* Church authority
and scriptural basis. Where finally doctrines, lacking
any scriptural warrant, come to prevail only in a later
age of the Church, and only partially then, like the
doctrine of the Immaculate Conception, or of Indulgences on the basis of the Treasury of Merits, doctrines

---

[1] If any one doubts whether the Eucharistic sacrifice is implied in Scripture, he should refer to Willis' *Sacrificial Aspect of the Holy Eucharist*.

[2] See Keble's *Letters of Spiritual Counsel* cxviii-cxxi.

[3] See Vincent of Lerins' *Commonitorium* on the trial of the Church which consists in the errors of single great churchmen (cc. 17 and 18).

ignored or rejected explicitly in the earlier ages, then, even without condemning them as positively heretical, we shall have no hesitation in declining them with emphatic decision.[1]

It is hardly possible to exaggerate the supreme importance of holding to nothing else than this ancient idea of the rule of faith as lying in the consent of the Church *and* the appeal to Scripture. After all, the Church's dogmatic decisions are rather negative than positive. They were passed in order to *warn us off* certain false lines of thought and development, while for positive information, for growth in spiritual knowledge, they still throw us back on the Christ of the Gospels and on the fresh teaching of the apostles. Thus it is only by keeping the whole surface of Scripture constantly before the eyes of the Church at large, that we can have amongst us the real mind of the

[1] I think these, with the Infallibility of the Pope, are the best test questions for the rule of faith. Take for instance the immaculate conception of the blessed Virgin. There is no passage in Scripture which even suggests more than her pre-eminent sanctity and beatitude. There is further no ancient consent even for her actual freedom from venial sins—no evidence at all of any one having held her immaculate conception. When the opinion arose in the Gallican Church of the 12th century, it is well known how St. Bernard denounced the festival instituted in honour of it, in the see of Lyons, and in the strongest terms repudiated the doctrine. His sentiments were constantly repeated by men of note and authority in the Church, and St. Thomas Aquinas summed up against the doctrine. Yet the opposite school has prevailed, and what was at first undreamt of, what Scripture does not hint at, what when it appeared, appeared as the opinion of a school repudiated by the greatest mediæval theologians, has finally been raised to the position of a dogma binding on the faith of every Catholic.

Spirit in all its richness and freedom, so that the Church can make fresh starts in view of new needs, so that she can bring forth out of her treasures things new and old, applying the old faith in new ways, because she is drinking constantly through her whole body at the original fount of inspiration. It is the complexity of our rule of faith—taking in the whole Church and the Scriptures and the individual, which is the gaurantee that the faith will not be centralized and narrowed, as it goes down the ages.

In the strength of such considerations we shall be better able to meet the reproaches which are sometimes aimed at us. For instance, we often hear much which would encourage the notion that the Church shows her vitality by the ready multiplication of dogmas, by the clearness and explicitness and frequency of her anathemas. We are far from minimizing the importance of dogmatic clearness: and we are far from denying that the English Church has had too little of it. But we must urge that a scriptural tone in theology, a scriptural spirit pervading all a Church's literature, is at least as essential a sign of healthy life, and there is a great deal in Scripture which puts a severe curb on the dogmatic temper.[1]

Further, let us not be alarmed when we are told that our rule of faith admits of no certainty. It admits indeed of as much certainty and definiteness, as a Christian who recognizes that truth is not coincident

---

[1] See on this subject some remarks in Mill's *Sermons on the Nature of Christianity* Serm. I. The scholastic dogmatists, resenting the reserve of mystery, simply explain away such utterances as that of Christ, St. Mark xiii. 32.

with dogmatic formulas can need to ask. Dogma is not a substitute for truth, but a guide to its apprehension. To accept a dogma on the Church's external authority is only the first step to apprehending it for ourselves. Indeed till 'dogma' has ceased to be a mere dogma, and become part of our own spiritual apprehension, we are not developed Christians, "spiritual men,"[1] and private judgment is only in error where it refuses to be enlightened by the catholic judgment. Scripture, the Church's mind, our own spiritual apprehension, are the three elements which must combine to produce in us the true holding of the Christian creed.

> "These are the three great chords of might,
> And he whose ear is tuned aright
> Will hear no discord in the three,
> But the most perfect harmony."

In conclusion let us explain in what sense we can believe the Church to be infallible. It is in the sense that the real mind of the Church is the Holy Spirit,[2] and where that mind is clearly expressed we can accept its guidance with confidence. It is expressed in her ecumenical creeds and dogmas about the central doctrines of the faith, and also with quite adequate clearness in her ordinary catholic teaching. But there is and has been a great deal *in* the

[1] 1 Cor. ii. 15.
[2] St. Thomas Aquinas like earlier Western teachers prefers the phrase 'I believe *that the Church exists*' to 'I believe *in the Church*.' But "if it is said 'I believe *in* the Holy Catholic Church,' this is to be understood in the sense that our faith is referred to the Holy Spirit who sanctifies the Church, so that the meaning is: 'I believe in the Holy Spirit sanctifying the Church.'" *Summa Theol.* Pars 2da 2dae Quaest. i. art. 9.

Church, that is not *of* her, for the Holy Spirit suffers in His organ, through men's unfaithfulness, and His voice speaks not always as plainly as He would fain let it speak, through human sin. Hence there has been a good deal taught in the Church, from time to time, that was not truth. If the truth has always been taught, yet it has sometimes been clouded by error. Indeed this imperfection in the Church's witness must be admitted by every thinking man. A Roman Catholic must recognize with us that a theory about Christ's ransom referred to just now—a theory at present almost universally rejected—was once for many generations almost universally held, and taught as part of the faith. He must admit that the Roman Church held through the Middle Ages, and taught authoritatively, a view of the 'matter' and 'form' of the Sacrament of Order now condemned. He must admit that the Gallican Church, and the Irish Church under its influence, repudiated for centuries the Papal Infallibility and described it as "no article of catholic belief." What does this mean? That on all showing the infallibility of the Church is not inconsistent with a great deal of error being also taught within her pale. To get at the Church's true mind we must not be content to accept the nearest or the loudest voice, but according to our opportunities "*inside the Catholic Church* we must look to the consent both of universality and antiquity, that we be neither carried away from sound unity to the side of schism, nor yet cast headlong from antiquity of religion into heretical novelties."[1]

[1] Vincent, *Common.* 29.

CHAPTER V.

THE PROMISE TO ST. PETER.

A PERSON anxious to arrive at the true conception of Church unity and Church authority, who had followed us thus far, might fairly urge that we had hitherto taken no account of some very remarkable words of our Lord to St. Peter. "The papal claims," such a person would urge, "are made to rest upon Scripture. They are made to rest upon the position assigned by our Lord Himself to St. Peter in relation to the whole Church, and upon the permanence of this relation in the ministerial succession."[1] To this promise of Christ to St. Peter, then, we will now turn our attention. St. Peter, acting as the spokesman of the other Apostles, had just given expression to the great conviction which had been slowly growing in the minds of the whole band, that the Son of Man was the Christ the Son of the living God. This outspoken confession of His Divine mission and Nature Christ meets and confirms with His most solemn benediction: 'Blessed art thou' (so we may venture to paraphrase it) 'Simon Bar-Jonah: for this conviction is not derived from weak human nature, it is a super-

[1] St. Matt. xvi. 13-20.

natural communication from above: and (in virtue of this thy profession of it) I also say unto thee that thou art Rock-man and upon this rock I will build my Church, and the gates of death shall not prevail against it. And I will give to thee the keys of the kingdom of heaven;[1] and whatsoever thou shalt prohibit on earth shall be prohibited in heaven, and whatsoever thou shalt permit on earth, shall be permitted in heaven.'

This passage is, on the face of it, one involving several ambiguities. It is difficult, I think, to feel any doubt that our Lord is here pronouncing the person Peter to be the Rock. The Church as a human society is to be built on human characters, and in virtue of St. Peter's courageous act of faith in Himself, his deliberate acceptance of His Divine claim, our Lord sees in him, what he had hitherto failed to find among men, a solid basis on which His spiritual fabric may be reared, or at least a basis capable of being solidified by discipline and experience, till it become a foundation of rock on which the Church can rest. So far our Lord is dealing with St. Peter as a human character, but He goes on beyond all question to promise

---

[1] *i.e.* the power of opening and shutting, and generally the office of the steward, see Isa. xxii. 20-22. On this expression and on the whole passage I must refer to what I have said elsewhere more at length—*The Church and the Ministry*, pp. 38 f. and 222 f. The underlying idea of the passage is admirably expressed by Mr. Holland *Creed and Character* p. 37 f. 'The Rock of the Church.

It is obvious to remark that the more we realize that Christ intended by 'the rock' the man Peter in his personal character, the less support can we suppose the passage to give to the Roman argument. This point was thoroughly argued in an article in the *Guardian* of May 22 1889 pp. 800 f.

to invest him with an office, the office of steward in the Divine kingdom, and with a supernatural legislative authority. So far our Lord's words bear a plain meaning, but after this we enter upon the region of ambiguity. St. Peter speaks in this passage as one of a body of twelve. Is Christ dealing with him as distinct from the others, or as their representative? Is the office to belong to him only or in a special sense, or is it to be given to all who share the apostolic commission? The ground for this question is left the more open by the fact that Christ is not here bestowing an office but promising it. The passage is an anticipation, a promise ('*I will*,' not '*I do*') which waits its interpretation in our Lord's future action, just as His discourse about 'eating His flesh' in St. John and His promise to 'give His flesh' (St. John vi. 51) waits its fulfilment at the institution of the Eucharist. We contend then that this is just one of those passages which want interpreting—one of those passages about the meaning of which it is not possible to arrive at any certainty without the aid of the interpretation, whether of Scripture itself or of the Church, which is given us to fix its meaning, positively and negatively, so far as it can be fixed.

The interpretation put on it by the modern Roman Catholic Church, involves two doctrines—first, a doctrine about St. Peter, and, secondly, a doctrine about the permanence of the Petrine position in the Church of all ages.

1. Our Lord here promised to constitute St. Peter, as the Rock of the Church, the supreme representative

of Christ the Rock. He is to be the Vicar of Christ to the Church on earth. To him alone is primarily given the pastorate of souls and the authority of the keys. To the other Apostles these are only given mediately through him. Whatever they have, they have not directly from Christ, but indirectly from Christ through Peter.[1]

2. Furthermore this position which St. Peter holds relatively to the whole Church, lives on in the Roman see in which St. Peter's 'privilege' abides unto the end, in the form of the universal pastorate and (as recently defined) infallibility, of the Bishop of Rome.

Now, without discussing the inherent probability of

[1] This position first finds expression in St. Leo *Serm.* iv. 2: "Great and wonderful, beloved, is the fellowship in Its own power which the Divine condescension gave to this man. And if It willed the other rulers of the Church to have anything in common with him, It gave only through him whatever it did not withhold from the others." cf. *Ep.* x. 1: "The mystery of this gift the Lord willed to belong to the office of all the Apostles in such sense as that He made blessed Peter, the chief of all the Apostles, the original depositary of it, and that He wills that from him as from a sort of Head, His gifts should flow down to the whole Body." The same idea is expressed by St. Francis de Sales in a passage quoted by Mr. Rivington *Authority* p. 28: "The Apostles all have the same power as St. Peter, but not in the same rank, in as much as they have it as delegates and agents, but St. Peter as ordinary head and permanent officer." The power of the Apostles relatively to Peter, is compared to that of representatives of a king relatively to the king. Fr. Richardson pp. 80-81 repudiates this mediatorial view. But my contentions would apply equally to the view which he accepts. The other apostles, according to him (quoting Allies), received jurisdiction directly from Christ, but in such sense that they could only exercise it in subordination to Peter as their head.

this interpretation (which is here stated very briefly, but not with any exaggeration of the claim made), and assuming simply, with what is almost excessive moderation, that the passage does not necessarily involve it, but is susceptible of others,—we propose to examine whether it can hold in view of the commentary on the promise which is afforded—

(1) by our Lord's own subsequent words and conduct:

(2) by the language of the Acts and Apostolic Epistles, including St. Peter's own:

(3) by the interpretations of the Fathers.

(1) It must, we think, be admitted that our Lord's subsequent language and conduct do not confirm the stronger and more exclusive meaning which has been put upon His promise to St. Peter. The solemn delegations of ministerial authority given by our Lord after His Resurrection, are so given as to imply the essential equality of all the Apostles. They positively exclude the 'mediatorial' position of St. Peter. "As the Father hath sent Me, even so send I *you*" the Apostles in general: "and when He had said this, He breathed on them and saith unto them, Receive ye the Holy Ghost; whosesoever sins ye forgive, they are forgiven unto them; whosesoever sins ye retain, they are retained." "All authority hath been given unto Me in heaven and on earth. Go ye therefore and make disciples of all the nations, baptizing them . . . teaching them." Thus the Mission to represent Christ, as endowed with His authority to baptize and to teach, to

remit and to retain sins (which is the power of the keys in its application to individuals) is given to the whole apostolic body at once and equally. To all equally had the Holy Eucharist been committed before His passion. It would seem then that what is promised to St. Peter in virtue of his confession of Christ's name, is bestowed by our Lord equally on all after His Resurrection, and that the primacy which St. Peter undoubtedly held in the apostolic college, carried with it no distinctive powers, but was a personal leadership amongst equals. There are indeed special dealings of our Lord with St. Peter. Thus before His Passion, when he is warning the apostles that 'Satan has asked to have them that he may sift them as wheat,' He tells Simon in particular that He has 'prayed for him that his faith fail not' and bids him 'when he is converted, to strengthen his brethren.' Mr. Rivington interprets this to mean that it was 'unnecessary' for our Lord to pray for all the Apostles because 'there was one head among them with whom they were to be joined': so that He prayed for one, in order to protect all! How strangely is this idea in contrast with the fact of our Lord's prayer in St. John, xvii. 9, 10. On this occasion the motive for His singling out St. Peter is plain to all who are not blind to facts. Thus St. Chrysostom commenting on this incident[1] says it is because his presumption, as indicated by his self-confident professions of loyalty, required rebuke... "He

---

[1] Tom. vii. p. 785 *Hom. in Matt.* lxxxii. 3, but there is a tendency to see in the charge 'strengthen thy brethren' a sign of Peter's primacy in *Hom. in Act. Apost.* iii., tom. ix. p. 26; but cp. on these Homilies, Salmon *Infallibility* p. 339.

said this sharply rebuking him, and showing that his fall was more grievous than the others and needed more assistance." "Why, if [Satan] asked for all, did He not say 'I prayed' for all? Is it not plain that it is as I said above—because He is rebuking him and showing that his fall is more grievous than that of the others that He turns His speech to him?" Again after the Resurrection Christ's threefold appeal to St. Peter and threefold pastoral charge, suggests irresistibly the interpretation given by the fathers,[1] viz. that St. Peter is here reinstated in the apostolic commission that his threefold denial might be supposed to have lost him; it is no peculiar dignity which is being committed to him. Thus St. Cyril of Alexandria: "through the thrice-repeated confession of the blessed Peter was annulled his sin in thrice denying: and through our Lord saying, Feed my lambs, there is conceived to be a sort of restoration of the apostolate already given to him."

Speaking generally then, we should say that the 'mediatorial' position of St. Peter in the ministry is excluded by our Lord's delegation of official power to all the Apostles directly, equally and together, and that there is nothing in the Gospels to suggest that St. Peter's position among the Apostles was any less personal or any more destined to be an abiding fact in the Church's ministry than that of St. John.[2] Even when our Lord

---

[1] *e.g.* St. Cyril *in loc.* and St. Augustin (substantially). So also St. Chrysostom, who however speaks here of St. Peter's primacy as the reason of his being singled out: see a little further on.

[2] On this subject we quote the following interesting passage from the end of St. Augustin's Homilies on St. John: "Two states of

was on earth it was not of a sort to prevent James and John asking for the foremost positions of honour in His kingdom, or the apostles discussing 'which of them is accounted to be greatest' (St. Matthew xx. 21; St. Luke xxii. 24).

(2) As we advance from the Gospels to the Acts of the Apostles, the history of the early Church suggests to us an obvious interpretation of St. Peter's primacy. He was the leader—the 'coryphæus' of the apostolic band. He spoke and acted at first as such, and, as holding

life, the life of faith on earth and the life of sight in heaven, were symbolized by Peter and John, the one by the one, the other by the other; but in this life they both of them walked for a time by faith [which Peter represents], and the other—sight [which John represents], they shall both of them enjoy eternally. For the *whole body of the saints,* therefore, inseparably belonging to the body of Christ, and for their safe pilotage through the present tempestuous life, did Peter, the first of the Apostles, receive the keys of the kingdom of heaven for the binding and loosing of sins; and for the same congregation of saints, in reference to the perfect repose in the bosom of that mysterious life to come, did the Evangelist John recline on the breast of Christ. For it is not the former alone, but the whole Church, that bindeth and looseth sins; nor did the latter alone drink at the fountain of the Lord's breast, to utter again in preaching those truths of the Word in the beginning, God with God, and those other sublime truths regarding the Divinity of Christ, and the Trinity and Unity of the whole Godhead, which are to be yet beheld in the kingdom face to face, but meanwhile till the Lord's coming are only to be seen in a mirror and in a riddle; but the Lord has Himself diffused this very Gospel through the whole world, that every one of His own may drink thereat according to his own individual capacity" (*In Ioh. Evang. Tractat.* cxxiv. 7).

St. Peter and St. John each represent, in their single personalities, among the Apostles, qualities and powers belonging to the universal Church. They stand as types of the Church in certain aspects, but the one embodiment is no more permanent than the other.

THE PROMISE TO ST. PETER.

'the keys of the kingdom of heaven,' opened the door to the Gentiles. But his position of leader does not seem to carry with it any prerogative of primary importance. The Apostles at Jerusalem are described as "sending him"[1] with St. John to Samaria. Later again he occupies no governing position in the Council at Jerusalem. Christ's revelation to him, indeed, when he opened the door to the Gentiles,[2] was a fact which must have been conclusive of the question before the meeting; but the formal authority, the formal " I decide,"[3] comes from St. James, and the decree goes out in the name of "the Apostles and elders"[4] generally.[5] Moreover, St. Peter retires into the background of history after this, as St. Paul rises into prominence. The history would seem to suggest that St. Peter's special function was one which had to do with the opening of Church history,[6] and this impression is augmented by the utterly 'unpapal' tone of St. Peter's own Epistles. The 'fellow-elder' who speaks to the other 'elders'

[1] Acts viii. 14.
[2] Acts xv. 7-11.
[3] Acts xv. 19.
[4] Acts xv. 23.
[5] Bishop Meurin in the controversy which originally gave rise to these papers interpreted Acts xv. 12 'all the multitude held their peace' "as an instance of the deference paid to St. Peter in the Council of Jerusalem, and had likened it to the present order of the Catholic Church, in which, when the successor of St. Peter speaks as such, on a matter of faith, the multitude hold their peace." This interpretation, which is common among modern Roman Catholics, is inconceivably misleading and perverse. The multitude held their peace for no other purpose than to listen to Paul and Barnabas.

[6] This is Tertullian's view (*de Pudicitia* c. 21), but his very powerful exposition is reduced in authority by the Montanist *animus* of the passage, which is aimed against the perpetuity of the power of 'loosing' in the Church.

but as a 'witness of the sufferings of Christ and a partaker of the glory that shall be revealed'[1] gives no hint that he stands in any special relation to the "Chief Shepherd" beyond that in which the other apostles stood.

As to the evidence of the rest of the New Testament, it goes very strongly in the direction of minimizing the position of St. Peter. The 'twelve foundations' of the Church equal and co-ordinate[2] are the twelve Apostles, and this implication of St. John's vision accords well with St. Paul's language.[3] Moreover, if one view can exclude another, St. Paul's assertion of his own essential apostolic independence,[4] and his language about the 'pillar Apostles,' *exclude* the idea of his receiving his authority in any way mediately from St. Peter, though his visit to him at Jerusalem was no doubt due to a

---

[1] 1 Pet. v. 1-4.
[2] Rev. xxi. 14.   [3] Eph. ii. 20.
[4] "Paul an Apostle not *from* man, neither *through* man" Gal. i. 1. "I did not receive it from man, nor was I taught it, but by revelation of JESUS CHRIST" i. 12. "They of repute" (*i.e.* the pillar Apostles, James and Cephas and John) "imparted nothing to me" ii. 6, etc. "The Gospel of the uncircumcision was committed unto me, as the Gospel of the circumcision was unto Peter" ii. 7. There is no sort of dependence of St. Paul on St. Peter which these words do not exclude. The Church officers of the next generation to the Apostles, like St. Timothy and St. Titus, received their authority and the tradition, not indeed *from* men, but *through* men. On the other hand the apostles received *immediately* from CHRIST. When Theodoret, wishing to please St. Leo, to whom he was appealing, speaks of St. Paul as "betaking himself to Peter that he might carry back from him an explanation to those who were raising questions at Antioch"— his language must have had a ring of irony to one as versed in Scripture as St. Leo.

certain deference to him as Captain of the Apostolic band.

We conclude, then, from our review of Scripture that the notion of St. Peter's 'mediatorial' position relatively to the other Apostles is excluded positively by St. Paul's language and conduct, and (by implication supporting this positive evidence) by the silence of the rest of Scripture as to any inequality amongst the Apostles. St. Peter's peculiar position, we should judge, given him in virtue of our Lord's promise, was a leadership in the Apostolic band which has its special exercise in the Church's earliest days, retires into the background with the spread and growth of the Church, and gives no sign of its being perpetuated any more than the special mission of St. Paul.

(3) It remains to summarize briefly the evidence of the Church Fathers on three points—(a) the meaning of 'the Rock' in St. Matt. xvi. 18; (b) the special position of St. Peter amongst the other Apostles; (c) the permanence of his prerogative in the 'see of Peter' at Rome.

(a) As regards the meaning of the Rock there is no fixity of interpretation amongst the Fathers, and many of them, like St. Augustin, give different interpretations in different parts of their works. Thus the comments of, say, St. Augustin and St. Chrysostom will convince any candid reader of what is certainly significant, namely, that they did not think the interpretation of this word a matter which at all affected the basis of Church authority, or indeed a very important question at all.

St. Chrysostom on St. Matt. xvi. 18 comments thus: "'On the rock' that is, on the faith of his [Peter's] confession," and passes on. But just below he speaks of God as having "made *a man that is a fisherman more solid than any rock.*" A little later[1] he speaks again of Christ having 'built his Church *on his confession.*' St. Augustin finally[2] bids his readers choose between the interpretation of the Rock as St. Peter, which was his earlier view, and Christ as confessed by St. Peter, his later. In the Collect for the Vigil of St. Peter and St. Paul in the Roman Breviary, the rock is interpreted of the apostolic confession 'apostolicae confessionis petra': in the hymn for Sundays at Lauds, on the other hand, Peter is 'ipsa petra ecclesiae.[3]

(*b*) As regards the position of St. Peter amongst the other Apostles we have statements from a number of the fathers. Thus Origen[4] writes: "But if you think the whole Church built upon Peter alone, what will you say of John, the son of thunder, or each one of the Apostles? And are we to dare to say that the gates of hell shall

---

[1] *Hom.* lxxxii. 3, tom. vii. p. 786.

[2] *Retract.* I. xxii.

[3] But the balance of Liturgical refs. to the passage, with which I have been kindly supplied by the Rev. F. E. Warren, goes in favour of the former interpretation.

[4] Mr. Allnatt (*Cathedra Petri* p. 30) quotes Origen as maintaining how highly St. Peter *transcends "the others" in power*. The words are put in capitals. The context when examined shows that "the others" means not the other Apostles, but the members of the Church generally, and that the point in which he transcends is having authority in "heavens" (plural) not in "heaven" (singular)

not prevail against Peter only, but that against the other Apostles and those who are perfect they shall prevail? Are not the quoted words, 'The gates of hell shall not prevail against it,' and 'Upon this rock I will build my Church,' said of them all, and of each single one of them? Are the keys of the kingdom of heaven given to Peter only, and shall no other one of the blessed men receive them? And if the words, 'I will give to thee the keys of the kingdom of heaven' are common to the others, how are not all the words, said before and said after, said as they seem to be to Peter, also common to the others? For in this place the words, 'Whatsoever thou shalt bind on earth, etc.,' seem as if they were spoken to Peter. But in the Gospel of John, the Saviour giving the Holy Spirit to the disciples by means of the Breath, says 'Receive ye the Holy Ghost,'" etc.[1] So again from Alexandria, Cyril, in one of his letters to Nestorius, which have ecumenical authority, speaks of Peter and James as of 'equal honour' as Apostles and disciples.[2] So much later Theophylact on Matt. xvi. 18-19: "They who have obtained the grace of the Episcopate as Peter had, have authority to remit and bind. For though the 'I will give thee' was spoken to Peter alone, yet the gift has been given to all the Apostles. When? When He said, 'Whosesoever sins ye remit, they are remitted.' For this 'I will give' indicates a future time—the time, that is, after the Resurrection."[3] St. Chrysostom very frequently recog-

---

[1] *in Matt.* tom. xii. 11.   [2] *ad Nest.* Ep. iii. 5.
[3] Tom. vii. p. 647 *in Matt. Hom.* lxv. 4: cf. tom. x. p. 329 *in 1 Cor. Hom.* xxxv. 5.

nizes the 'primacy' of St. Peter, and calls him "the chief of the apostles, the mouthpiece of the disciples, the leader of the band."[1] He speaks of St. John and St. Paul 'allowing him the primacy.' But this cannot be strained to imply any essential difference of rank, for where he speaks of St. Paul as going up to visit St. Peter, on account of this primacy, he adds "not as needing anything of him nor of his voice, but as being his equal in honour."[2] So he constantly speaks of St. Paul as 'the teacher of the world,' and characterizes St. John 'as the pillar of the Churches over the world, having the keys of heaven."[3]

In Western theology the only definite view given us of St. Peter's relation to the other Apostles (till we come

---

[1] Tom. viii. p. 525 *in Ioan. Hom.* lxxxviii. 1: ἔκκριτος τῶν ἀποστόλων καὶ στόμα τῶν μαθητῶν καὶ κορυφὴ τοῦ χοροῦ. Here he distinguishes 'the apostles' from 'the disciples.' Just below where he says "He intrusts to him [Peter] the presidency of the brethren . . . and says, 'If thou lovest me preside over the brethren'" he means 'the brethren' to represent 'the sheep' of Christ *i.e.* the flock generally. Where lower down he speaks of him (p. 527) as appointed by Christ 'the teacher not of this see (of Jerusalem) but of the whole world,' it is by contrast to St. James who received only 'the throne of Jerusalem.' The term 'coryphaeus' he applies also to Andrew, James, and John, who make up 'the two pairs of coryphaei.' (*Hom. in Matt.* xxxvii. 4; tom. vii. p. 420.) It is noticeable that when he is speaking of the election of Judas' successor he mentions three possible methods of making it. St. Peter might have asked Christ to give him a successor to Judas simply: or the apostles might have elected simply: or St. Peter might have chosen some one himself, see *Hom. in Act. Apost.* iii. 1; tom. ix. pp. 23-25.

[2] *in Gal.* i. 18; tom. x. p. 677 ἰσότιμος ὢν αὐτῷ.

[3] Cf. *in Gen. Hom.* xxxii. 3; lx. 3; xxiv. 4; tom. iv. pp. 320, 581, 222. For St. John cf. *In Ioh. Hom.* i. 1; tom. viii. p. 2; cf. tom. vii. p. 368.

to the 'mediatorial' theory, referred to above as belonging to the Papacy and derived from Leo the Great) is that propounded and developed in the African Church by her great theologians St. Cyprian, St. Optatus, and St. Augustin. This theory may be briefly stated in St. Cyprian's language. It is, that while "the other Apostles were what Peter was, endowed with an equal fellowship both of honour and power," while "the Lord after His resurrection gives equal power to all the Apostles" and gives them all equally the pastoral commission, yet He built His Church upon one (Peter), to "make the unity of His Church plain."[1] This institution of the Church in the person of one man first, was a symbolic act to emphasize Christ's intention of unity. Peter, when Christ speaks to him, after his great confession, is addressed (as St. Augustin often says) as the "representative of the Church." This is an interpretation of our Lord's words to St. Peter which we can all accept, and which is quite intelligible. It is quite distinct from the mediatorial view, according to which St. Peter is something which the other apostles are not, and the source to them of what they are. This latter view is indeed markedly excluded by the language of the fathers generally, except indeed by those like St. Leo who constitute what can be truly called the "papal school" of writers.

(*c*) It remains for us to inquire what is the patristic view about the *permanence of St. Peter's privilege* in his see. On this subject it is not necessary to say much now, as it will come under discussion in the next chapter

[1] *De Unit.* 4.

on the growth of the Roman see. For the present it is only important to make one point clear—that the claim of the Bishop of Rome to be what Peter was among the Apostles becomes a claim which, even if recognized, does not carry us far when we have once gained a true conception of what Peter was among the Apostles. The exaggerated claim which we hear through the lips of Leo, and which has been referred to above, is based on a conception of St. Peter's position the unfoundedness of which we have already seen. Meanwhile, even when this claim has been reduced to its proper limits and made only a claim to be among bishops what Peter really was among Apostles, even so the claim of the see of Rome to the 'Privilege of Peter' cannot show anything approaching ancient *consent* in its favour. Allnatt in his *Cathedra Petri* can at least be trusted to accumulate all the legitimate references to the Fathers in support of a papal view—indeed he does not often stop here—but under the heading "*St. Peter lives and teaches in his successors*" and "*rules in his own see*" he cannot quote a single Father of the first four centuries, except one pope, Siricius (A.D. 386); and under the head of "*the see of Peter*" he cannot quote a single *Oriental* Father of the first four centuries,[1] except indeed Firmilian of Caesarea, who is violently protesting against Pope Stephen's conduct, presumably based upon his claim to sit in Peter's chair, and mentions the claim without expressing his own attitude towards it: "Stephen who

---

[1] *e.g.* St. Chrysostom in his voluminous works, including letters to the Pope, affords no testimony, though he speaks often of Peter's 'primacy' among the other apostles.

announces that he holds the see of Peter by succession is stirred by no zeal against heretics."[1] I believe indeed that *none of the Greek Fathers of the first six centuries connects the position of the Bishop of Rome with the promise to St. Peter.*[2] In the African Church the theory that the Bishop of Rome occupies that same position as the 'symbol of unity' in the whole Church, which St. Peter occupied in Apostolic days, came to prevail through the influence of St. Cyprian. This interesting view, which in St. Cyprian's sense we should be heartily glad to accept, will come under discussion shortly. For the present the matter must be brought to a close with two observations.

There is a marked contrast between the authority which such a doctrine as the Real Presence of Christ in the Eucharist can plead, and that which supports the papal view of the 'privilege of Peter.' We accept the Real Presence because (*a*) it was taught by the Fathers of East and West from the first; (*b*) it is confirmed by the natural meaning of our Lord's words, and the language of St. Paul in his epistles. We reject the papal interpretation of Christ's promise to St. Peter, because (*a*) it cannot show in its favour anything approaching to a consent of the fathers— indeed there is something much nearer consent in a

[1] ap. Cypr. *Ep.* lxxv.
[2] This position was suggested to me, and I cannot find any instance to the contrary. (Even from later days the instances seem very rare, and rather by way of casual implication. Theophylact on St. Luke xxii. 32 says simply that Peter by the example of his penitence is to 'strengthen his brethren' to the end of time.) But a universal statement is somewhat hazardous.

view which excludes it; (*b*) it does not appear to be the obvious meaning of our Lord's words at first, and is rendered still more improbable by His later language; (*c*) it is excluded by St. Paul's language about his own authority, discountenanced by the general language of other New Testament writers, while it cannot even plead anything in the New Testament, outside the Gospels, in its support.

It is undoubtedly true that the papacy has possessed itself of the promise of our Lord to St. Peter in popular imagination, just in the same way as Protestantism of an un-catholic sort has possessed itself of certain portions of St. Paul's epistles about justification by faith, and the superiority of the spirit to the letter. Thus there are a number of texts about which we start with a kind of 'false conscience,' which we have to deal with, not (as we are apt to do) by avoiding them, but by dealing with them with attention and prayer, in the light of the mind of the Church, of the general sense of Scripture, and of the reason which God has given us and His Spirit enlightens, till we are familiarized with their true meaning and it has taken its proper place in the context of our catholic faith.

CHAPTER VI.

THE GROWTH OF THE ROMAN CHURCH.

IT is important for us, at the present stage of our argument, to have before us a clear historical summary of the position occupied by the see of Rome in the successive ages of the Church, such a historical summary seeming an essential condition of any sound judgment as to what our relation towards the Roman Church ought to be.

The earliest Father then who mentions the subject, St. Irenaeus, regards the Roman Church as having been founded concurrently and equally by St. Peter and St. Paul. In fact, (as we find from St. Paul's Epistle to the Romans) there was a considerable body of Christians at the capital before any Apostle had been amongst them,[1] but St. Paul was amongst them during his first and second captivities, and St. Peter was at Rome probably when he wrote his First Epistle—certainly before his martyr's death, which he shared there with St. Paul, perhaps in A.D. 67.

The prominence in which the Christian Church of

[1] Rom. i. 11, 12. St. Paul had not seen them, and he would not go where any other Apostle had been before him (xv. 20, 21). St. Peter must have come to Rome at any rate not much before the end of St. Paul's first captivity, in A.D. 63.

the capital of the world must have inevitably found herself among other Churches, the glory which accrued to her from her apostolic and other martyrs,[1] and not least, the early munificence of her almsgiving, gave the Roman Church a special position in Christendom from the earliest days. Attention has been called to the fact that when she writes the Epistle which bears St. Clement's name in order to exhort a recalcitrant party in the Church at Corinth to submission to their presbyters, she writes with a tone of considerable authority.[2] "If any disobey the words spoken of God through us, let them know that they will entangle themselves in transgression, but we shall be clear from this sin." "You will cause us joy and exultation if, obeying the things written by us through the Spirit, you cut out the lawless passion, etc." This tone of authority may be due to the prestige of the Church at Rome;[3] but it seems more likely that, though the letter is written in the name of that Church, the authority is mainly St. Clement's, and that he speaks with authority as one of the chief order—the apostolic order of bishops—writing to a Church in which as yet there were no officers higher than presbyters.[4] But in any case it is remarkable that

[1] "That happy Church" Tertullian calls her "for which the Apostles poured out with their blood their whole teaching" (*de Praescr.* 36).

[2] c. 59. The epistle was written about A.D. 95.

[3] "St. Ignatius" says Mr. Allnatt "writes to the '*presiding*' Church of Rome": Yes, 'presiding,' but where? "In the place of the region of the Romans," and there too "having the presidency of love."

[4] See this discussed *The Church and the Ministry* p. 324, cf. p. 329.

THE GROWTH OF THE ROMAN CHURCH. 95

the episcopate seems to have been less prominent in the Church at Rome than was the case in the East.[1]

It is towards the end of the second century, when the line of Roman bishops comes into clearer historical light, that we begin to discern dimly the first beginnings of their claim to be successors of St. Peter; and it is in A.D. 196, in the person of Victor, that we have our first anticipation of the aggressive spirit which is to be a distinguishing characteristic of the see of Rome in later ages. Victor ventured in a domineering spirit to excommunicate the Asiatic Churches who held to their Johannine tradition and insisted on keeping Easter on the day of the Jewish passover, whatever day of the week that might be. This arbitrary act on Victor's part brought down upon him the 'sharp rebukes'[2] of a number of bishops, and amongst them of the great St. Irenaeus, who contended that variety in ecclesiastical custom had never hitherto been a bar to fellowship, because such 'difference only serves to commend the unity of the faith.' Victor stood reproved. His excommunication failed. It was a mere 'attempt'—not in the sense that he did not actually issue the sentence, for Eusebius tells us that he did; but simply because it was ignored, and the question of Easter observance

[1] Thus Dr. Salmon *Introd. to N. T.* p. 565 *n.* calls attention to the fact "how all through the first two centuries the importance of the Bishop of Rome is merged in the importance of his Church." Cf. Lightfoot *Clement* i. p. 70: "the later Roman theory supposes that the Church of Rome derives all its authority from the bishop of Rome, as the successor of St. Peter. History inverts this relation, and shows that, as a matter of fact, the power of the bishop of Rome was built upon the power of the Church of Rome."

[2] See Eusebius *Hist. Eccles.* v. 24.

remained an open one till the Council of Nicæa closed it. The attempt however is significant of a spirit already in its slight beginnings present in the Roman Church. And it is important to notice that Eusebius, the fourth century Church historian, sees in Victor's action nothing but a piece of undue intolerance. He acknowledges nothing 'papal' in the bishop of Rome.

It would not appear that any kind of authority was attached to the Roman see during the early centuries even in the West, except such moral authority or prestige as must have belonged inevitably to so great an apostolic see. With reference for instance to the Church's function of bearing witness to the faith, the voice of the see of Rome is but one element in the consentient testimony.[1] But yet her position in this respect has one remarkable feature, due to her relations to the capital city of the world. Rome was the centre of the world's movements. Everybody came thither. She was the world's 'microcosm.' It followed necessarily that she stood, as regards her Church, in a unique freedom of communication with the Churches of the rest of the world. Christians from all parts necessarily gravitated thither. The faith in Rome was not only preserved by the local Christians, but tested by constant comparison with the faith of those who like Hegesippus or Polycarp came from widely different quarters to the world's centre and testified to finding there the same faith as they had believed at home. Thus it was that the testimony of the Roman Church had a 'microcosmic' character; and when Irenaeus wants to

[1] See Tertullian *de Praescr.* 36. St. Irenaeus iii. 3.

select a typical Western[1] Church in order to enumerate the succession of her bishops and 'confound' the Gnostics with her creed, he chooses as a specimen, because "it would be tedious to enumerate the successions of all the churches," the Church of Rome: "for to this Church on account of her superior pre-eminence, it must needs be that every church should come together, *that is, the faithful from all sides*; and in this Church the tradition from the Apostles has been always preserved [not as elsewhere by a merely local body but] *by men from all parts.*"

At an unknown moment, before the middle of the third century, the Church of Rome, which up to that time had been Greek in language—alike in her liturgy and her theology—a Greek colony in the Latin city, became perhaps somewhat suddenly a Latin Church, and in consequence of this change of language, so com-

---

[1] He balances Rome in the West with Smyrna in the East. This passage from Irenaeus (iii. 3.) has been the subject of much dispute. I believe that Dr. Langen, following Grabe and Neander, has finally fixed its meaning (*Gesch. der röm. Kirche* i. 172 note). He quotes new and apposite illustrations, from twelfth-century Western writers, showing how the words of Irenaeus 'convenire ad Romanam ecclesiam' were then understood. Thus "Roma tunc erat caput mundi et de toto orbe illuc conveniebant" (Herveus of Bourgdieu) "ad quam homines undique terrarum conveniunt" (Hugo Eterianus). We may compare the language of the *Synodicon* of Constantinople, which attributes the primacy of the older Rome to the fact that formerly "affairs converged there and therefore all men came together there" (Milman *Lat. Chr.* ii. 127). No interpretation is tenable which does not give force to the remarkable words I have italicized. The popular Ultramontane interpretation is excluded by its violating the whole context: cf. Salmon *Infall.* pp. 376-7; Puller *Primitive Saints and See of Rome*, pp. 31-43.

98   THE GROWTH OF THE ROMAN CHURCH.

pletely forgot her Greek past that in the fourth century she was ignorant of an incident in her life which the coincidences of modern discovery have laid open to our eyes. This incident we notice here only so far as it illustrates with remarkable vividness the position of the Roman Church in this, till recently, unknown epoch of the early third century. St. Hippolytus, the great theologian and bishop[1] of the Church, "who perhaps' says Dr. Newman "has no rival (among ante-Nicene theologians) except his master St. Irenaeus," is in his *Refutation of all Heresies* now discerned denouncing his contemporary, Pope Callistus, with extraordinary violence, as a destroyer of the Church discipline and indeed (to quote Dr. Newman again) as 'a heresiarch ex cathedra.' Now it is a luminous fact that a great theologian can call a bishop of Rome a heresiarch without seeing any more significance in the fact than he would see in the case of the bishop of any other see, and without his attitude towards him affecting the universal reverence in which his name was held, "which a breath of ecclesiastical censure has never even dimmed." This incident, which we cannot but reckon a fact of history, illustrates how little essentially ecumenical there was in the position of the Roman see at this date, and how utterly alien to the mind of the greatest Roman theologian of the third century was

---

[1] The theory of St. Hippolytus' position which is perhaps the most probable, is that he was 'bishop of the nations,' *i.e.* bishop of the foreigners in the diocese of Rome, taking his title from Portus. See Lightfoot *Clement* ii. pp. 332 ff.

any sort of notion that could even remotely point to the doctrine of Papal infallibility.[1]

Leaving for the next chapter the task of tracing the development of the papacy in Latin Christianity, we proceed now to notice that in the doctrinal and disciplinary system of the Eastern Church the position of the Roman see remained where it was in the conception of Irenaeus. The pre-eminent position of the see is of course recognized, as when the Churchmen of the East complain to St. Dionysius of Rome of the suspicious teaching of St. Dionysius of Alexandria, "because the first of bishops was the person to whom complaints against the second were most naturally carried,"[2] but if either the universal pastorate of the bishop of Rome or, *a fortiori*, his infallibility is put forward as having a claim to be part of the Church's catholic Christianity, such a claim can be shown to be untenable in the light of facts.

Let us consider two or three of these facts.

When in the extreme crisis of the conflict for the Nicene faith the Pope Liberius "subscribed to heretical depravity" (so St. Jerome speaks of his signing a compromising creed), abandoned Athanasius and notified

[1] I may refer on this subject to the *Dict. Chr. Biogr.* s.v. HIPPOLYTUS ROMANUS vol. iii. pp. 88-91, 96. Dr. Newman *Tracts Theol. and Eccl.* p. 222 would apparently regard the passage in the *Elenchus* about Zephyrinus and Callistus as an interpolation. But this is most arbitrary. "I grant" he says "that that portion of the work which relates to the Holy Trinity as closely resembles the works of Hippolytus *in style and in teaching*, as the libellous matter which has got a place in it is *incompatible with his reputation.*" [The italics are mine.]

[2] Robertson's *Church History*.

that he had separated him from his communion, St. Athanasius betrays no other feeling than that of sorrow at the fall of a good man and anxiety to palliate his weakness: "he speaks with a noble tenderness of the fall of both Liberius and Hosius" (of Cordova). Now we contend that if anything in the world can be certain, it is certain that St. Athanasius, had he had any idea of the bishop of Rome being in a unique sense the guardian of the faith, much more any notion of his infallibility, must have adopted another tone in regard to his fall. He must have quivered at the awful shock of finding himself deserted by the 'Holy Father' on the central dogma of the faith. It must have been much more to him than his desertion by Hosius. There is no avoiding or palliating this conclusion.

The impression made upon our minds by this incident is deepened by the evidence of the general Councils. The attempt to foist into the history of the Council of Nicæa any sign of a belief in the universal pastorate of the bishop of Rome is violent in the extreme.[1] The fathers in their 6th Canon recog-

---

[1] We cannot help quoting the following paragraph from the work of one of the most learned of English Roman Catholic historical writers—Allies' *See of St. Peter* (p. 155). "In the year 325, at the great Nicene Council . . . it is stated 'that the Roman Church always had the primacy.'" [This clause (*a*) originally meant the primacy in her own region (*b*) was a *Roman interpolation* in the acts of the council, expressly disallowed by the East, and rejected even by respectable Roman authorities, such as Hefele.] "The bishop of Corduba, in Spain, apparently at once papal legate and imperial commissioner, and Vitus and Vincentius, legates of S. Sylvester, presided over the Council." [It seems impossible to ascertain exactly who did preside over the Council.

THE GROWTH OF THE ROMAN CHURCH. 101

nized in Rome a quasi-patriarchal power in her own region like that which they acknowledged equally in Alexandria and Antioch. They recognized nothing more. And we must go further. The fourth ecumenical Council, at Chalcedon, A.D. 451, following on the lines of the second, makes a canonical statement (Can. xxviii.) about the authority of the see of Rome which shows their view of the matter with unmistakable clearness :—

"The fathers properly gave privileges to the throne

Hosius may have done so, but that he was papal legate comes only on the authority of a confessedly romancing historian of no weight and of the later fifth century, Gelasius of Cyzicus, and that Vitus and Vincentius did so, is not hinted by any authority at all.] "And it was determined that all these things should be sent to Sylvester, bishop of Rome, for his confirmation, which only could make the Council ecumenical." [This statement comes (*see* Hefele *Conciliengeschichte* i. 426) from Dionysius Exiguus, and represents nothing more than the "Roman view" at the beginning of the 6th century.] Thus to ignore all contemporary sources of information and to compile narratives from the fictions of late or romancing authors is the Ultramontane way of writing history. In the same spirit Mr. Rivington makes a reference to a passage in Sozomen p. 42. "Inasmuch as the care of all belonged to him (*i.e.* Julius, bishop of Rome), on account of the rank of his see he restored to each (of the Oriental bishops who had been driven away with Athanasius) his Church." This is from Sozomen *E. H.* iii. 8. But the word translated 'inasmuch' means more strictly 'on the plea that.' It represents Julius' view of his authority, and Mr. Rivington curiously enough has not gone on to quote Sozomen's account of how the orientals dealt with his claim to authority. "They wrote back a letter full of irony and not without stern threatening . . . they did not choose to take the second place . . . they complained of Julius having insulted their synod . . . they repudiated what had been done as unjust and contrary to the rule of the Church." Nor did Mr. Rivington mention that Sozomen's account of Julius' claim, as tested by his own letters, is exaggerated. See *Athanasius' Hist. Writings* (Bright) *Pref.* p. xxvii.

of old Rome, because it was the imperial city, and the 150 Bishops (at Constantinople), being moved with the same intention, gave equal privileges to the most holy throne of new Rome (*i.e.* Constantinople), judging with reason that the city which was honoured with the sovereignty and senate and enjoyed equal privileges with the elder imperial Rome, should also be magnified like her in ecclesiastical matters, being the second after her."

So spake the fathers of Chalcedon in the teeth of the protest of, the legates of Rome. Nothing can be more certain than that the bishops who enacted this canon did not regard the privileges of Rome as part of the divine and essential constitution of the Church or they could not have used the expression "the fathers gave": nothing can be more plain than that the primacy of Rome is in their eyes a 'primacy of honour.'[1] Jealousy of the growing claims of Rome may have had something to do with the tone of the canon—with its silence about the *spiritual* dignity of the see of St. Peter; but its language cannot do less than disprove the idea that the claims which Rome was even then beginning to make were regarded by the Eastern Church as part of the catholic faith. Further, this canon explains in what sense, and in what sense only, the Council, in the complimentary letter in which they endeavoured to persuade St. Leo to accept their 28th Canon, can address him as "ruling like a head

---

[1] See the expression 'privileges of honour' in the 3d Canon of Constantinople to which that of Chalcedon refers back its authority. On the whole subject Dr. Bright's admirable *Notes on the Canons* should be consulted. "The Quinisext Council, 681, confirmed all the Chalcedon canons without exception." Salmon *l.c.* p. 417.

THE GROWTH OF THE ROMAN CHURCH. 103

over the members" in the Council, and "commissioned by Christ with the guardianship of the vine."[1] It is quite true that individual oriental bishops, especially appellants to Rome who wished to say what was pleasant, and men like St. Cyril of Alexandria, whose fear of the rising claims of Constantinople united his interests with those of Rome, recognized from time to time in a higher sense the universal pastorate of the Roman bishop,[2] but their expressions belong to individuals only, under circumstances when interest put strong pressure on belief. There is nothing of the sort to be found in St. Basil's or St. Chrysostom's voluminous works, though this belief, had it existed in their minds, must have emerged: and more than this—oriental writers are much given to verbose compliments in addressing distinguished people. The language of rhetoric and compliment must always be interpreted by the severer style of a formal canon.

Once again, whatever strong language may be quoted from a few later oriental writers on behalf of the Roman see, as from St. Theodore the Studite in the 8th century, nothing can override the evidence of the formal

---

[1] In fact any committee might address its president as "ruling like a head over the members." The 33d Apostolic Canon is very much to the point: "The bishops of each nation (race) ought to recognize the first amongst them and esteem him as a head, and do nothing over and above (their proper business) without his judgment."

[2] Though St. Cyril in the early years of his episcopate preferred remaining outside the communion of Rome to restoring St. Chrysostom's name to the diptychs of the Alexandrian Church, and Theodoret in spite of his language in addressing Leo, which was referred to in the last chapter, signed with a voluntariness which he emphasized the 28th canon of Chalcedon.

action of the 6th General Council in 680, when it condemned Honorius the Pope among the Monothelite heretics. "With them we anathematize" says the Council "and cast out of the Holy Catholic Church, Honorius, who was pope of the elder Rome, because we found that he followed Sergius' opinion in all respects and confirmed his impious dogmas." Roman Catholic writers may endeavour to justify the actual language of Honorius, they may protest that the contemporary pope never intended to assent to his condemnation except for *negligence in opposing heresy*,—we are not concerned at present with these contentions[1]—but no one can possibly, with any show of reason, contend that the insertion of the name of the pope in a list of formal heretics by an ecumenical Council, does not prove that the bishops who composed the Council had no, even rudimentary, idea of the papal infallibility.

Here then we leave the matter. The only claim here made is to have demonstrated one fact—that the belief in the universal pastorate and the doctrinal infallibility of the pope can in no sense be described as part of the catholic faith; it cannot by any stretch of terms be described as part of the creed of Christendom held *ubique, semper, ab omnibus*. Therefore, on the principles laid down already, it cannot be part of the obligatory creed of Christendom at all. Short of this there is very little we should not be prepared either to grant, or at least to leave an open question. We are not disposed

---

[1] See Willis' *Pope Honorius and the New Roman Dogma. Papal Infallibility inconsistent with the condemnation of a Pope for heresy, etc.* (Rivington, London, 1879.)

at all to question the unique position held in Western Christendom by the see of Rome. We are not disposed to minimize the magnificence of the vocation assigned to her, especially in view of the Church's need of centralization in the days when the Western Empire was decaying or gone. We would fain not fall short of what is fitting in our veneration of the greatest of Christian patriarchates. But no such veneration can justify us in assenting to *any* claims she likes to make, or in shutting our eyes to the fact that the acceptance of these claims is only possible on the basis either of a 'Manichean' disbelief in the capacity of the human reason to estimate the plainest facts of history, or of a doctrine of development which would cut at the root of the patristic principle that, in the rule of faith obligatory upon Christians, "whatever is truly new" or really partial, "is certainly false."

CHAPTER VII.

THE DEVELOPMENT OF THE PAPACY IN LATIN CHRISTIANITY.

No one can fairly contemplate the greatness of the papacy or consider how vast a position it occupies in the whole of history, without being satisfied that it is something greater than could ever have been created by the ambition or power of individual popes or by the evil forces of injustice and fraud. It is one of those great historic growths which indicate a divine purpose latent in the tendencies of things and the circumstances of the world. A Leo, a Gregory, a Hildebrand could no more have devised or invented the papacy, than a Cæsar, a Constantine, or a Justinian could have elaborated the Roman Empire. It is a natural development of circumstances, and it is in the fashioning of circumstances that we look for the hand of Providence. In the fourth and fifth centuries the fact that the Western mind was comparatively undisturbed by the oriental heresies in regard to the Person of Christ which occupied the great ecumenical councils, caused the Western Church, and the great see which was the acknowledged centre of the Western Church, to seem to the eyes of the distracted orientals as a perpetual harbour of quiet refuge. Rome in her dignified repose was the recipient of appeal after appeal from the East. Further, though the Roman Church was not a great theological centre, like Antioch or Alexandria, or like the African Church among Latin-speaking peoples, and later the Church of South Gaul, yet in proportion as she was lacking in theological power, she was endowed with a splendid capacity for "holding the tradition" with unswerving orthodoxy. Individual Popes did indeed fail, and at important crises, like Liberius and Honorius, but on the whole the orthodoxy of the see of Rome was conspicuous through all the controversies on the Trinity and the Incarnation. The consequent enhancement of her general ecclesiastical reputation coincided with the deeper sense of the need of a recognized centre to Western Christendom which finds expression in the canon of Sardica. And while the Roman see was thus having greatness thrust upon her from the circumstances of the Church's position, the tendency of events in the secular world was running steadily in the direction of her exaltation. The decay of the Western Empire and the removal of the seat of government from Rome, left the magnificent traditions of authority and the splendid prestige of the eternal city to add lustre to the chair of St. Peter, whose occupants became constantly more important as paganism died away and each Western emperor was more contemptible than the last. Once again, the age which saw the crumbling of the old civilization of the Empire and the surging in of the great sea of fresh and vigorous barbarian life, in wave after wave of invasion, cried out, in the interests of society as much as of religion, for some centre of moral and social authority; and men's eyes had long grown accustomed to look upon Rome as the centre of the social system.

"Now" says Dean Milman, speaking of the age of Gregory the Great—" Now was the crisis in which the Papacy must re-awaken its obscured and suspended life. It was the only power which lay not entirely and absolutely prostrate before the disasters of the times— a power which had an inherent strength, and might resume its majesty. It was this power which was most imperatively required to preserve all which was to survive out of the crumbling wreck of Roman civilization. To Western Christianity was absolutely necessary a centre, standing alone, strong in traditionary reverence, and in acknowledged claims to supremacy. Even the perfect organization of the Christian hierarchy might in all human probability have fallen to pieces in perpetual conflict: it might have degenerated into a half secular feudal caste with hereditary benefices, more and more entirely subservient to the civil authority, a priesthood of each nation or each tribe, gradually sinking to the intellectual or religious level of the nation or tribe. On the rise of a power, both controlling and conservative, hung, humanly speaking, the life and death of Christianity—of Christianity as a permanent, aggressive, expansive, and to a certain extent uniform system. There must be a counterbalance to barbaric force, to the unavoidable anarchy of Teutonism, with its tribal, or at the utmost national independence, forming a host of small, conflicting, antagonistic kingdoms. . . .

It is impossible to conceive what had been the confusion, the lawlessness, the chaotic state of the middle ages, without the mediæval Papacy; and of the mediæval Papacy the real father is Gregory the Great."[1]

There is, then, in the deepest sense of the words a providential purpose in the papacy, and it is impossible to estimate all that the Church as a whole owes to the great see of Rome. But of course we recognize a providential purpose of a not dissimilar kind, and in relation to the spread of Christianity, in the growth of the Roman Empire and the diffusion of the Greek language. We recognize a divine vocation given to the Eastern Church as the great mother of theology, as least as conspicuous as that which was intrusted to the West in the sphere of discipline and government. But this recognition does not carry with it either of two important consequences. It does not carry with it any recognition of a dogmatic authority given either to East or West in isolation, nor does it carry with it any implication that the vocation we recognize is part of the Church's unalterable system. Any vocation which is rooted in the circumstances of a particular epoch may vanish with the circumstances which conditioned it. It does not follow because governmental authority or centralization was the one thing needed in the seventh century that it is the one thing needed now: what is the very symbol or instrument of unity in one age may be the source of schism in another, and the Divine Providence which gave its vocation first to Greek and then

[1] *Hist. of Latin Chr.* b. iii. c. vii. vol. ii. pp. 100-102 ed. 1883.

to Latin Christianity may have as great a vocation in store (who can tell that it may not be so?) for the English-speaking and Oriental Churches. At any rate we go no way towards recognizing whatever claims Rome may choose to make upon us, when we allow ourselves in unstinting admiration of the greatness of the work which God has allowed her to do; for it is true of everything in Christianity, as in the world at large, —of everything which is not part and parcel of her catholic system doctrinal, moral, and sacramental—that

> "The old order changeth, yielding place to new,
> And God fulfils Himself in many ways,
> Lest one good custom should corrupt the world."

And when we come to look a little closer at the history of the Roman Church it seems to us to have all the appearance, taking it in general, of a system, backed indeed by a divine intention, but perverted by something which is much more satanic than divine. We know that St. Peter Damian called the great Hildebrand his "sanctus Satanas," and the expression, in whatever sense originally used, has a very striking application to the papacy as a whole. The certainly very undivine qualities of ambition, injustice, and dishonesty have been to a strange extent identified with the whole history of the papacy. These qualities are all the more conspicuous when we see them in so real a saint as the man who has a claim to be called the father of the papacy, Leo the Great. Saint as he was, he was wonderfully unscrupulous in asserting the claims of his see, and strangely blinded in conscience to the authority of truth when he quoted, as a canon of Nicæa, what had been shown to demonstration to be a canon of Sardica and not of Nicæa.[1] Again, we may not be able to fix on any individuals the responsibility for such forgeries as the Donation of Constantine and the Isidorian Decretals, but it goes against our surest instincts to believe that a system, which was corresponding in its actual method of working to a divine purpose, could have been allowed to depend so largely upon forgeries for its substructure at critical epochs, as the Roman system has in fact depended.

Nay, even *conscious* fraud is a familiar element in official acts of the Roman see.[2] And further, the

[1] *Leo the Great* (Fathers for English Readers) pp. 113-115.

[2] See *e.g.* Willis' *Pope Honorius* p. 26: "The condemnation of Pope Honorius for heresy is recorded in the Roman Breviaries until the sixteenth century; at which period the name of Honorius suddenly disappears. The theory of Papal Infallibility was at that time being rapidly developed. A fact opposed it. The evidence for the fact is suppressed. 'I have before me' writes Père Gratry 'a Roman Breviary of 1520, printed at Turin, in which, on the feast of S. Leo, June 28th, I find the condemnation of Honorius: In which synod were condemned Sergius, Cyrus, Honorius, Pyrrhus, Paul and Peter . . . . who asserted and proclaimed one will and operation in our LORD JESUS CHRIST.

"'I open the Roman Breviary of to-day,' he continues, 'and there I find in the instruction of S. Leo (June 28th): In this Council were condemned Cyrus, Sergius and Pyrrhus, who preached only one will and operation in CHRIST. The trifling incident of a Pope condemned for heresy by an Ecumenical Council is simply omitted by the revisers of the Breviary in the sixteenth century. Father Garnier, in his edition of the *Liber Diurnus*, says, with a gentle irony, that they omitted it for the sake of brevity.'"

See also his quotation of Father Gratry's letter, p. 28. "Has GOD, then, need of your falsehoods, that you speak deceitfully for Him? 'Numquid indiget Deus mendacio vestro, ut pro eo loquamini dolos?' This mode of apologetics without openness is love of interpolations and falsifications is alive still among Roman controversialists. The interpolations in St. Cyprian are still printed as an integral part of the text by Father Hurter[1] and quoted by Allnatt[2]; and perhaps there is nothing which gives to the minds of intelligent and truth-loving men so invincible a prejudice against the Ultramontane system and temper—nothing which so radically convinces them that it is not divine—as the certainty that Ultramontane writers will

one of the causes of our religious decay for centuries past. As soon as human nature perceives in the apostle the smallest trace of craft or duplicity, it turns aside and takes to flight; the best always flee farther than the rest. Their souls do not listen to the voice of liars : 'Oves non audiunt vocem alienorum.' What then, are we—we catholic priests, ministers of Jesus Christ and of His Gospel, and servants of His Church? Are we the preachers of falsehood or the apostles of truth? Is not every truth, every true gift, every historical and real fact for us, just as every falsehood is against us? Has not the time arrived—in this age of publicity, in which everything is seen and brought to light, in which everything that before was spoken in the ear, is now preached upon the housetops—has not the time arrived, I repeat, to reject with disgust the frauds, the interpolations, and mutilations which liars and forgers, our most cruel enemies, have been able to introduce amongst us? . . . . I myself was long before I could believe in this apologetic of ignorance, blindness, and half-honesty, or rather dishonesty, which desires the end, which believes in the goodness of its aim and its truths; but which, to attain this end, has recourse to deceit, to mystery, to force, to falsehood, to a fraudulent invention of forged passages. Once more, Has GOD need of these frauds? . . . O ye men of little faith, of low minds, of miserable hearts, have not your cunning devices become the scandal of souls?"

[1] *Sanctorum Patrum Opuscula Selecta* vol. i.

[2] *Cathedra Petri* pp. 40-41. He defends the interpolations by the analogy of the text of 'the heavenly witness' (1 St. John v. 7, 8); as if we would quote that in defence of Trinitarian doctrine!

always be found manipulating facts and making out a case, will never behave as men who are loyally endeavouring to seek the light and present facts as they are.

If the actual history of the papacy prevents us from regarding it as a growth in accordance with the will of God, at least as forcibly does it prevent us from considering the claim it has recently made, to be part of the Christian Revelation, or—what the Vatican Council declared it to be—a 'dogma divinitus revelatum.' It is indeed to 'triumph over history' for the Pope to assert that in decreeing his infallibility he is "faithfully adhering to the tradition received from the first beginnings of the Christian faith." The doctrine of the Papacy is so manifestly a gradual growth by accretion that no one can possibly, with his eyes upon the facts of history, regard it as part of the faith 'once for all delivered.' That the evidence of the Eastern Church will not permit of our accepting as catholic any of the later papal claims has been already shown. It remains to show that in the West also the papal doctrine is of the nature of an occasional growth.

In the fourth century, the Western Church at the Council of Sardica formally allowed an appeal on the part of condemned bishops to Julius of Rome.[1] Their third

[1] In the third century there is an interesting instance of an appeal first to Rome, and then away from Rome to Cyprian. The circumstances were briefly as follows. Two Spanish Bishops, Basileides and Martial, had denied the faith in the Decian persecution, and either resigned their sees or been deposed. Successors had been duly appointed when they visited Rome and, under false pretences, induced the Pope Stephen to take up their cause. Accordingly he took some steps to promote their restoration. Under these circumstances the Spanish Churches appealed to

canon runs as follows: "The bishop Hosius said . . . .
If any bishop in any matter seems to have been condemned [unjustly] and supposes himself to be not unsound, but that his case is good for a renewal of the trial: if it please your charity, let us honour the memory of the apostle Peter, and [direct] a letter to be written by the bishops who have tried the case to Julius bishop of Rome, so that the case should be heard again if it be necessary, by the bishops near the province in question, and that he may himself appoint the judges." Here and in the two following canons which form the basis of the appellate jurisdiction of Rome, the bishops of the West appear not as recognizing an existing or essential right, but as conferring a privilege, in view of certain experienced needs—just as the bishops in a Pan-Anglican Conference might find it necessary to institute a right of appeal to Canterbury in honour of the memory of Augustin. When in the case of the African presbyter Apiarius, the Roman bishops quoted these canons of

Cyprian and sought his aid, and Cyprian, in company with other African bishops assembled in the synod of Carthage in A.D. 254, addresses a letter to them strongly affirming the validity of the new consecrations, and apologizing for Stephen's mistaken action on the ground of his distance from the scene and ignorance of the true circumstances. See Cyprian *Ep.* 67. Baronius *Annales* A.D. 258 § v. expresses a 'vehemens suspicio' that Rome must have had a last word in the matter, and this 'suspicion' has become a fact in Gröne *Papstgeschichte* i. p. 58 (Regensburg, 1875). He describes out of his own imagination how the Spanish deputation, after receiving Cyprian's sentence, went to Rome and obtained a reversal of the previous judgment. He then describes the whole incident as "a speaking proof of the primacy of the Roman bishop." The facts, as history records them, are in truth suggestive of the natural, non-theological, manner in which the system of appeals grew up.

Sardica, as canons of Nicæa, and used them to justify interference with the ordinary jurisdiction of an African bishop over his presbyter, the Church of Africa first ascertained by consulting the oriental authorities that these canons were not Nicene, and proceeded in council[1] to guard jealously the rights of their own Church and to repudiate the papal interference : " We find it enacted in no council of the fathers that any persons may be sent as legates of your holiness. . . . . Do not therefore, at the request of any, send your clergy as agents for you, lest we seem to introduce into the Church of Christ the ambitious pride of the world."

The Papal authority is thus, at its root, a growth of circumstances, not a part of a revelation. So again if we examine the language of the theologian of the fourth century who is sometimes quoted as an extreme partisan of the just-developing papal claim—St. Jerome, it will be very evident that 'what he recognized in Rome is recognized rather in the way of personal predilection than of ecclesiastical doctrine. When he is bewildered amid the confusion of theological disputes in the East, he throws himself upon the authority of the Roman bishop, as he sits aloof in the calm security of the West. " Following no one as chief but Christ" he writes to Pope Damasus "I am associated in communion with your Blessedness, that is with the chair of Peter. On this rock I know the Church was built." " Define, I beseech you, if it pleases you, and I will not fear to speak of three hypostases. If you bid, let a new creed be established after the Nicene, and let

[1] A.D. 425.

us who are orthodox confess our faith side by side with the Arians in similar words." " I meanwhile keep crying out: Whosoever is joined to the see of Peter is mine."[1] This language seems clear enough, but apparently later in life, after he had abandoned Rome in disgust, he can adopt exactly the opposite tone. 'The custom of the Roman Church' he says in effect 'has no more authority than the custom of any other church. The episcopate at Rome has no more authority essentially than any other episcopate.' "If it is a question of authority, the world is greater than the city. Wherever there is a bishop, at Rome, or at Eugubium, or at Constantinople, or at Rhegium, or at Alexandria, or at Tanis, he has the same worth (meritum), the same priesthood. The power of wealth or the humility of poverty do not make a bishop higher or lower. They are all successors of the Apostles."[2] This passage is

---

[1] *Epp.* 15, 16. One cannot fail to catch the tone of exaggeration almost of irony in the second of these passages. It is perhaps worth noticing that the phrase against which Jerome was protesting so strongly ('tres hypostases') and in his protest against which he had the Pope and the Western Church on his side, after all came to be the accepted phrase.

[2] *Ep.* cxlvi. I have given reasons for dating this letter in the later part of Jerome's life in *Church and Ministry* p. 172 n.[1] The context of the words quoted may be explained thus. St. Jerome after a certain period in his life is zealous in maintaining the dignity of the priesthood of the presbyter, as against the arrogance of bishops and, on the other hand, the self-assertion of deacons. Thus in this epistle he is maintaining in effect that bishops are substantially of the same order as presbyters, only differing in the power of ordination. But the 'custom of the Roman Church' is pleaded against Jerome. At Rome the bishop on the one hand occupied a unique position, and the deacons, on the other, who were only seven in number, occupied a more dis-

not quoted by Roman controversialists, for a very plain reason: because it indicates that the authority of the Roman see rested for Jerome on what is variable in a theologian—on sentiment, on expedience, on feeling —not on what is invariable, the basis of doctrinal authority.

Once again, the theory of the see of Peter held by the African theologians of the third and fourth centuries, while it makes the Roman see amongst other Churches the symbol and normal centre of unity, as Peter was amongst the Apostles, does not involve any distinctive *authority* in the Roman bishop. The see of Peter is the symbol of that episcopacy in which all bishops equally share, which inheres in its entirety in each episcopate, and *renders each bishop fundamentally independent* and responsible for his actions to none but God.[1] This

tinguished position than the presbyters of whom there was a 'crowd.' Jerome treats this plea with great contempt. "If it is a question of authority the world is greater than the city." A bishop is everywhere substantially the same. As for the deacons "Why do you produce against me the custom of one city? . . . Everything is more desired where it is rare. Among the Indians fleawort is more precious than pepper."

[1] "There is" cries Cyprian "one God, and one Christ, and one Church, and one see founded on Peter by the voice of the Lord" (*Ep.* xliii.), but he is asserting not the claims of the see of Rome, but of his own see of Carthage. The see of Peter is equivalent to the episcopate. Fuller references on St. Cyprian's theory of the episcopate will be found in *The Church and the Ministry* p. 165 f. But I may refer here to the expression in *De Unitate* 5: "the episcopate (in the Church) is one, and is shared by each bishop in such a way that he is responsible for the whole" (or "that the whole is held by each"—*a singulis in solidum pars tenetur*). On this basis the independence of each bishop is frequently stated. "Each bishop exercises in the administration of his Church the free choice of his own will, having to give account of his action to

is the theory as St. Cyprian states it. He regarded the see of Rome (as being in a special sense the see of Peter) as the normal centre of unity, but not as the centre of unity in any such sense as would enable it to impose conditions of communion which interfered with the catholic liberty of other Churches. This however was exactly what Stephen of Rome endeavoured to do. He went so far as to excommunicate St. Cyprian and the African and Oriental Churches which agreed with him, for refusing to recognize the validity of heretical baptism—a matter on which there had been no ecu-

the Lord" (*Ep.* lxii. 3). The see of Rome is described (*Ep.* lix. 14) as "the see of Peter, the principal Church, whence sacerdotal unity had its origin," but these last words can only mean that Peter's episcopate was the first given, or (as Puller *Prim. Saints* p. 56 interprets) that the African succession was derived from Rome. In the very context of this expression he goes on to reassert the independence of each episcopate.

I think it is in place to notice here the evidence of a tract "on dice-players" (*de Aleatoribus*) commonly printed with Cyprian's works. It is plainly written by a bishop, and as he speaks of the divine goodness having bestowed upon him the "leadership of the apostolate," "the vicariate of the Lord," "the original authoritative apostolate on which Christ founded his Church" (c. 1, apostolatus ducatus, vicaria Domini sedes, origo authentici apostolatus) he has been supposed, by Bellarmin and others, to have been bishop of Rome. The evidence however is against this hypothesis: it appears to be by an African bishop of the third century. And in any case it must be noticed that the titles mentioned above are titles not of the papacy but of the episcopate. The 'we' of c. 1 is explained in c. 2 as "we, that is we bishops, shepherds of the sheep" "since we bishops have by the laying on of hands received the same Holy Ghost (as came upon the Apostles) within the shelter of our breast." Thus "the leadership which belongs to the apostolate" "the vicariate of the Lord" "the original authoritative apostolate" are titles of the *episcopate* as such. Indeed that every bishop represents Christ is a commonplace of the theology of Ignatius and of early Church writers in general.

menical decision,—and no language can be more forcible than that in which both Cyprian and Firmilian assert their own episcopal independence against what they regarded as the arrogant claim of St. Stephen. Thus St. Cyprian's own attitude towards St. Stephen interprets his language about the Roman see with a vivid clearness. Nor did St. Augustin in later days see in Cyprian's conduct in this matter anything but what deserved the highest commendation.[1] If Optatus, who was earlier than Augustin, seems to attribute to the see of Peter at Rome more actual *authority* as the centre of unity, it must be remembered that he too uses 'the see of Peter' in an ideal sense as identical with the episcopate, and if he is emphatic on the necessity of union with the see of Peter he is as emphatic on the necessity of union with the Asiatic Churches, to whom St. John wrote.[2] Both the see of Rome and the Churches of Asia are in different senses the symbols of catholic unity.

Thus if we examine the history of the Western Church, we do indeed find a high position assigned from very early days to the see of Rome, considered as in a special sense the see of St. Peter. But we do not find anything which justifies its later claims, still less anything which justifies these claims being regarded as part of the

[1] He modifies indeed St. Cyprian's language about the independence of the individual bishop. But the authority which he recognizes as limiting the freedom of the individual bishop is that of the General Council.

[2] "Outside the seven Churches," he says, speaking of the Asiatic Churches with whom he and the Catholics are in communion, "whatever is without, is alien" (*De Schism. Donat.* ii. 6, again vi. 3). No one can read the Epistles to the Galatians or Corinthians who is not in communion with those Churches.

catholic heritage of the Church. No doubt after the fifth century the history of the Western Church is mainly the history of the exaltation of the papacy. Isidore of Seville [1] no longer interprets the injunction to St. Peter "feed my lambs," as the typical pastoral charge to feed the little ones of Christ's flock. The 'lambs' are now the bishops of the churches of the world whose government is by a special charge committed to Peter and his representatives. Nevertheless the growth of the claim of Rome and of its acceptance was slow, gradual, and intermittent. St. Gregory the Great can repudiate [2] as pregnant with satanic arrogance the title of "universal bishop" which afterwards appears in the forged decretals as a papal title and which so clearly describes the papal claim. The popes of the seventh century acquiesce [3] in pope Honorius' letter being subjected to the judgment of a general Council, and submit to, and accept, his condemnation, and for many centuries each pope on his accession condemned among formal heretics one of his predecessors.

[1] *Ep.* viii. c. A.D. 620.
[2] It is remarkable how the words which Gregory uses (*Epp.* l. viii. 30) when he is repudiating this title—"meus honor est honor universalis ecclesiae"—have their meaning reversed when they are quoted in the Vatican decree. Gregory meant by them: 'I wish for no honour which detracts from that of other bishops. Their honour is mine.' He goes on "if you (the Bp. of Alexandria) call me universal pope, you deny that you yourself are what you confess me to be, universal. But away with such an idea. Let an expression be heard no more which inflates pride and wounds love." In the Vatican decree (cap. 3) the words are quoted in the sense that the Papal honour communicates itself to the subordinate bishops and does not interfere with their jurisdiction. [3] See Willis' *Pope Honorius etc.*

The Forged Decretals represent a step of immense importance in the aggrandizement of the papal claim. It is not that they contain a wholly new claim, but they converted what was a claim, a pretension, an aspiration, into an accepted principle firmly rooted in the precedents of the whole Christian past, reaching back to the Apostles. For what were these Decretals? They were a forgery of the middle of the ninth century, and the first part consisted of a number of decretal letters supposed to be by the early Popes from A.D. 90 to 314. These forged letters represented these bishops of Rome as claiming and exercising the rights of the mediæval Papacy. "The fraud consisted in assigning the language of a later period to the writers of an earlier one." Thus their recognition gave to the growing claims of the Papacy an altogether fallacious appearance of antiquity. No sober historian can deny that this successfully inaugurated a wholly new epoch of canon law. It is impossible to exaggerate the extent to which they elaborated and strengthened the system of appeals to Rome and developed the existing tendency to centralize the governmental authority of the Churches in the hands of the Pope. "The reforms," says the Jesuit Père Regnon, "brought about by the Pseudo-Isidore consisted in reserving to the Roman pontiff the trial and judgment of all bishops."[1]

But the Papacy of these Pseudo-Isidorian decretals only represents a stage in an upward progress. The papal

[1] Quoted by E. G. Wood *Regal Power of the Church*, whose pages on this subject should be consulted: cf. also "Janus'" treatment of the subject pp. 94 ff.

pretension, which grew always with the growth of actual power, reached its extreme point as far as the claim of authority is concerned in the Bull *Unam Sanctam* of Boniface VIII., A.D. 1302.[1] The authority here claimed is absolute and universal in the secular and spiritual spheres alike. But the day of decline, at least for a time, was at hand. The reforming Councils of Constance and Basle (A.D. 1415 and 1432) assert in the strongest language the subordination of the Pope to General Councils. "First of all" so ran the decree of Constance "this Council declares that inasmuch as it is legitimately assembled in the Holy Ghost, constituting a general Council, and representing the Catholic Church militant, it has its power immediately from Christ, and that all men of every rank and dignity, even the Pope, are bound to obey it in matters pertaining to the faith, and the extirpation of the above-mentioned schism, and the general reformation of the Church of God in the head and the members." And the decree goes on to denounce condign penance and punishment, on even a pope who should venture to disobey the decrees of the Council. These decrees were passed without a single dissentient voice. Their language "leaves no doubt that they were understood to be

[1] Quoted in Gieseler (*Eccl. Hist.* iii. 146) who throughout summarizes clearly the stages in the growth of the papal claim. I suppose that the attitude of practical devotion towards the vicar of Christ encouraged among Roman Catholics exceeds the bounds even of the theory. Cardinal Patrizi in a document "addressed" (as is remarked in the *Dublin Review* April 1865 p. 440) "to the Catholics of Pius IX.'s own diocese, by his express sanction and under his very eye," claims for the Encyclical of that Pontiff and, consequently, for every like expression of the Pope's mind, to be the *very word of God*, to be received on pain of forfeiting heaven.

articles of the faith, dogmatic definitions of the doctrine of Church authority. And they deny the fundamental position of the Papal system."[1]

The Pope however on the whole triumphed over the Councils. A Papal reaction set in. And if no general claim since made can exceed that of the *Unam Sanctam*, at least the claim of doctrinal infallibility emerged into greater distinctness, as the logic of events demonstrated the untenability of the theocratic claim over the world. But the doctrine of papal infallibility was the opinion of a school only, not a dogma. It was repudiated with the most genuine earnestness up to a quite recent date, as for example by the Anglo-Roman body in 1789 and by the Irish Bishops in 1810,[2] or in a document as common as Keenan's *Controversial Catechism* where it was declared to be "no article, of Catholic belief."[3] Thus nothing can be more certain than that the fully developed Papal claim is the result of a very gradual and intermittent growth. It is

[1] "Janus" *The Pope and the Council* p. 302. See for the decree Creighton *Hist. of the Papacy* i. p. 291 and app. 16.

[2] See Gladstone *Vaticanism* pp. 44-49. He mentions also that the eminent Roman Bishop Baines declared in 1822 that 'he did not believe any Catholics in England or Ireland maintained the Infallibility of the Pope.'

[3] Keenan's *Controversial Catechism or Protestantism Refuted and Catholicism Established* Ed. 1846, with the imprimatur of the Vicars-apostolic for Scotland. P. 117 *of the Powers of a General Council*, etc.: "Must not Catholics believe the Pope in himself to be infallible?" "This is a Protestant invention; it is no article of the Catholic faith; no decision of his can oblige under pain of heresy, unless it be received and enforced by the teaching body— that is, by the bishops of the Church." [In later editions this section is omitted.] The Constitution *Pastor aeternus* declares on the other hand that "it is a dogma divinely revealed that the

124 THE DEVELOPMENT OF THE PAPACY.

in fact not a *development* of the original idea of the Episcopate, so much as a subversal of it. The original ideal of the Episcopate would have secured for the Church a duly representative government, and would have provided, by the confederation of relatively independent Churches, a system of checks upon one-sided local tendencies. The Papacy represents the triumph of imperial absolutism over representative, constitutional authority, and of centralization over consentient witness and co-operation. It was indeed a lamentable 'triumph over history' when Pius IX. declared that in decreeing the Papal Infallibility a "dogma divinely revealed" he was "faithfully adhering to the tradition received from the first beginnings of the Christian faith."[1]

Roman Pontiff, when he speaks *ex cathedra* . . . is possessed of that infallibility with which the Divine Redeemer willed that His Church should be provided for defining doctrine regarding faith or morals : and that therefore such definitions of the Roman Pontiff are irreformable of themselves, and not from the consent of the Church."

[1] Some of the 'difficulties' in the way of believing in the infallibility of the bishop of Rome, apart from the question whether it is an article of the catholic faith, have been noticed above in *e.g.* the failure of Liberius, and the condemnation of Honorius as a heretic. There are others however of overwhelming magnitude, especially the apparently and intentionally dogmatic utterances of Popes on the different sacraments, which have turned out erroneous. Thus Nicolas I. assured the Bulgarians that Baptism in the name of Christ only was valid. *Resp. ad consult. Bulgar.* 104. Labbe *Collect. Concil.* ix. 1566. Nicolas II. compelled Berengarius to acknowledge the Capernaite heresy that Christ's body is *sensibly* (sensualiter) touched by the hands and broken by the teeth in the Eucharist. Eugenius IV. in his instructions to the Armenians makes the 'porrection of the instruments' the essential matter of the Sacrament of Order. These are in fact only examples.

CHAPTER VIII.

THE NATURE OF SCHISM.

IF it be granted that enough account has already been given of what constitutes the Church's unity of Life, and of what is necessary for her unity in the Truth, yet there still remains to be dealt with, that third sort of unity which was referred to at starting as characterizing the Church. This is the unity of Love, or outward fellowship, 'the bond of peace,' which it is so fully our duty to preserve that wilful schism would annul all the moral fruits which follow from being constitutionally within the ecclesiastical unity. That is to say—schism does not merely mean breaking away from the episcopal form of government. The schisms of the early Church were episcopal in form, but none the less they were understood to put their responsible members outside the Church's saving unity.[1]

What then constitutes the guilt of schism? Not merely being separated, for the separated party may not be the guilty party, as, for example, in the case when Diotrephes 'excommunicated' the brethren who came from St. John,[2] or Pope Victor the Asiatic Churches, or

---

[1] St. Cyprian 'On Unity' was written against *episcopal schismatics*.   [2] 2 St. John 9, 10.

Pope Stephen St. Cyprian and the African Churches. None of these excommunicated parties were understood to be schismatics. Schism, considered apart from heresy, as a sin excluding from the benefits of church life, means *wilful self-withdrawal from the legitimate succession of the catholic Church* on the part of an individual or party, or, in a secondary sense, the *wilful causing of a breach inside the Church.*

Schism is a state of things which results generally from one of two tempers of mind. It may be the result of the pride which will not brook ecclesiastical subordination, which makes men stand upon their dignity, and resent some supposed slight or injury because they value their own self-esteem above the Church's fellowship. It was this sort of self-assertion and the personal animosity which springs from it, which produced the schism of Felicissimus at Carthage against St. Cyprian, and it has played a large part in the history of modern divisions. It is easily understood that schism so bred, should generally involve heresy, for the self-will which isolates itself to avoid unpleasant subordination is not likely to miss the temper of self-opinionatedness in matters of faith, and we understand St. Jerome's words—"no schism fails to devise a heresy for itself to justify its withdrawal."

But schism may have what we must call a nobler root. It may spring from impatient, undisciplined zeal against evil in the Church. The zealous reformer smarts with indignation against the abuses and undiscipline which deface the Body of Christ. He and his followers are afraid to contaminate themselves by connivance with that which they cannot quickly alter. Their zeal is too much for their reverence for Christ's plan, for their subordination, for their patience. They take the matter of God's Church into their own hands. They deal with it, with more or less of recklessness, in their own way. The temper of reverent caution which fears to dispense with, or lay hands upon, outward forms, whether of divine appointment or reverend antiquity, because for the moment their practical value is obscured—this is forgotten or discarded by the men of intemperate, impatient zeal; and thus they form a Church of their own with a righteousness of their own, and a constitution of their own choosing. This is the second source of schism in the Church. If we consider the causes of the great presbyterian schisms of the Reformation, how undisciplined, how unguarded do we find to have been the zeal of their main authors! Or to go further back, what else was the root of the disciplinary schisms in the early Church—of Montanism, of the schism which Novatian created at Rome, of the schism of the Donatists, of the schism of Lucifer, of the schism at Antioch against St. Meletius? Can we not directly trace Tertullian's development among the Montanists into a schismatical attitude towards the Church to that tone of intellectual and moral impatience which characterized his whole mind, and which he himself deplores when he writes *On Patience*, "as an invalid who, since he is without health, knows not how to be silent about its blessings," "as one ever sick with the heats of impatience must of necessity sigh after and invoke and persistently plead for that health of patience which he possesses not." This impatience which Tertullian deplores in himself was the animating spirit in the whole body of disciplinary schismatics.

But from whatever cause it may spring, schism—episcopal or not—is unequivocally condemned by the fathers. "It were better to endure anything," said St. Dionysius of Alexandria to Novatian, "than to break up the Church of Christ; martyrdom to avoid division were no less glorious than martyrdom to avoid idolatry; nay, in my judgment were more glorious." "The sin of schism," says St. Cyprian, "seems to be worse than failing to confess Christ in persecutions." "There is nothing more serious than the sacrilege of schism," says St. Augustin. "No such reformation," says Irenaeus, "can be effected by them, as will compensate for the mischief arising from their schism." "It is no less an evil than heresy," says St. Chrysostom.

On one or two of the ancient schisms it is necessary to say something more in detail. First, on Donatism: because (since the days of Dr. Newman's 'Apologia' at any rate) it has been the fashion to compare the condition of the Church of England with that of the Donatists. Let us make an imaginary story of events in England which would bring the facts of the English Church in the sixteenth century into exact analogy to those of Africa in the fourth, and the imaginary case will show us both what sort of conduct would have really constituted an English protestant episcopal schism, and also how far in fact the English Church is from being implicated in anything of the sort. Suppose that a body of zealous reformers in the reign of Mary, despairing of the Church of England, had, on the election of an archbishop of Canterbury, raised frivolous objections against him, consecrated a rival prelate first to that see, and then in a number of other places; established a separate Church in England, and gathered large numbers of adherents; declared itself not only the only Church of England, but the only Church of the world, the catholic Church having ceased to exist through the contamination of evil; suppose, we say, such a course of action had been pursued, and that the schismatical Church had succeeded in gaining the majority in England for a while and subsisting side by side with the catholic succession, baptizing, as persons not yet Christian, those who came over to them from the catholic Church; then you would have had a parallel to the Donatist schism. Be it ever remembered that the Donatist body in Africa was not constituted by a reform of a national Church, but was as distinct a schism *from* the Church of their own district, as ever took place: and that the Donatist body held itself the only true Church of the world,—in both points differing *toto caelo* from the position of the Anglican communion.

We have avoided entering into the details of the Donatist history to save space, but of the details of the schism at Antioch something must be said, as it illustrates an important principle—that there can be schism *in* the Church as well as a schism from the Church—a schism in the Church, leaving both separated parties within the communion of the Church catholic.

The schism at Antioch, then, dates from the withdrawal of an orthodox party in the fourth century from the ministrations of an Arian prelate. This withdrawal met with the approval of St. Athanasius and his friends; but the public profession of orthodoxy by the bishop, Meletius, who had been elected under Arian auspices, gave the separated body an opportunity to return into communion with him. All seemed in train for a restoration of unity when the intemperate and hasty action of Lucifer—a firebrand among prelates, who afterwards organized a schism of his own—perpetuated the breach, by giving the orthodox party a separate bishop, Paulinus. There was a great deal of the schismatical spirit of impatient zeal in that action which left the Antiochene Church with rival prelates and rival bodies of adherents, but the most strenuously orthodox party in the Church at large could not bring themselves to disown Paulinus. He was accepted by Rome, by Alexandria, by the West, while the East generally held to St. Meletius. Remaining thus unrecognized by Rome as Bishop of Antioch, St. Meletius notwithstanding presided till his death at the second Council accepted as ecumenical in the Church, and has been acknowledged since his death as a saint both in East and West. We may then quote as appropriate to the case of St. Meletius a remark of the Roman Catholic historian Tillemont with reference to some later Eastern saints of the period of the Monophysite schism (who lived and died out of the communion of Rome because they remained in communion with Acacius, the patriarch of Constantinople, who was excommunicated by the Pope). "As Elias and Flavian had always remained in communion with Acacius by the fact of their continuing in communion with Constantinople, the Pope Hormisdas [at the restoration of unity] did his best to secure their exclusion from the diptychs of their Churches. But their people preferred to submit to the extremest measures rather than do this injury to the memory of those who had been their glory while they lived. So much so that the Roman Church was obliged to do some violence to her own maxims: she seems in fact to have at last abandoned them by honouring, as her protectors in heaven, those whom she would not admit to her communion on earth."[1] The Antiochene schism is, therefore, significant as illustrating some facts of importance: that there may be a schism with faults on both sides, even in a local Church, when neither side is finally regarded as out of the communion of the Church at large: that there are circumstances when even a somewhat schismatical act like that of Lucifer may be condoned: that breaches of fellowship *in* the Church do not necessarily always involve breaches of communion *with* the Church. Nothing in fact can be called schism in the full sense of the word except conscious self-withdrawal from that part of Christ's visible and orthodox Church to which one belongs, and to neither of the Antiochene parties is this act attributable. In this local separation then we mark the distinction between breaches *in* the Church and separation *from* the Church.

It is very possible to construct an imaginary parallel

[1] *Mem. Eccl.* xvi. 708. I think it is not without importance to notice that the language of the Roman liturgy still involves the idea that the Church is divided and requires corporate reunion: she prays our Lord 'to bring her into peace and unity (pacificare et *coadunare*) according to His will.'

in Reformation history to the case at Antioch. Supposing the English bishops in Elizabeth's reign had become heretical, and an orthodox party retaining communion with the West had withdrawn from their communion: supposing the Anglican bishops, say in James I.'s reign, had returned to orthodoxy, while almost simultaneously a rival succession of bishops was established over the separate body—in such rival successions you would have a parallel to the state of things at Antioch. It is hardly necessary to remark that this parallel *is* imaginary, because the state of things was not as we have supposed. But such a schism might have left both parties with a fair claim to represent the Church catholic in England.

We have established hitherto two principles:—that there is such a sin as schism which in and by itself is sufficient to unchurch a community; and, secondly, that short of this, there is such a thing as a breach of communion *in* the Church, which is due to the 'old leaven' working in her—the temper of schism militating against the temper of love. A little consideration and reading will show that the separation of East and West and the separation of England and Rome[1] were not due to conduct which constitutes schism in the primary sense of the term—not, that is, to self-withdrawal from the Church catholic; but that they *were* due to that temper of schism which is always at work

---

[1] I shall return to this subject again, but it may be needful, even now, to recall to the reader's mind the fact that the English Church has never excommunicated the Roman Church, but the Roman Church her.

and, like sin in any shape, mars the manifestation of God in the Church at large.

In the party spirit in the Church of Corinth St. Paul sees the schismatical temper. In Victor's conduct when he excommunicated the Asiatic Church for not keeping Easter after the common fashion, Irenaeus would lead us to see the same temper, which is ready to violate the unity of love for something which falls short of the necessities of the faith.[1] Once again, when Pope Stephen endeavoured to excommunicate Churches which held the invalidity of heretical baptism (an opinion which no general church voice had yet condemned), he was anticipating the due action of church authority in the interests of his own see and in the temper of impatience to deal with what he thought disastrous. Pride in the cause of a man's own see, intolerance, impatience, these are notes of the schismatical temper. This is what was plain to St. Cyprian and St. Firmilian, the most conspicuous amongst the bishops attacked. They accuse St. Stephen of intolerable arrogance in interfering with the liberty of other episcopal sees. St. Firmilian says very boldly that the Pope 'is the true schismatic,' and has 'cut off' from communion none other than 'himself'[2]—meaning that the temper of schism, and, therefore, the guilt of schism lies not with those who are unjustly excluded, whether by 'Diotrephes, who loveth to have the pre-eminence, and casteth the brethren out of the Church,' or by any other bishop, but with him who does the unjust act in the interests of ambition or impatience. And we should

[1] Euseb. *H. E.* v. 24.   Cypr. *Epp.* lxxii.-lxxiv.

notice St. Augustin's verdict upon St. Cyprian in this matter, where he so strongly asserted the independent rights of his see. He praises him (to the Donatists) as the very type of the unschismatic temper. Why? Because, unlike the Donatists, even in a matter of such great importance as the validity of heretical baptism, he did not press the opinion which the African Church then legitimately held (for it was still an open question); he did not go beyond the limits of ecumenical authority; he did not excommunicate those who held the validity of heretical baptism, but bore with them in a matter where the universal Church's voice was not distinct. "Cyprian and those with him walking in most persistent tolerance, remained in unity with those who taught differently from them." "Though they held that heretics and schismatics did not possess baptism, yet they chose rather to have communion with them when they had been received into the Church without baptism . . . than to be separated from unity; according to the words of Cyprian—'Judging no one and depriving no one of the right of communion if he differ from us.' . . . Behold, I see thus in unity Cyprian and others his colleagues, who on holding a council decided against the validity of baptism given outside the Church. But again, behold, I see in the same unity that certain men think differently in this matter, and do not dare to re-baptize. All of these catholic unity embraces in her motherly breast, bearing each other's burdens in turn, and endeavouring to keep the unity of the spirit in the bond of peace until the Lord should reveal to one or other of them if in any point they think otherwise than as they should."[1] Unity, St. Augustin here says with great distinctness, is in a sense to be preferred to truth of opinion. That is to say, to violate the unity of fellowship on behalf of an opinion which may be tenable or true, but is not authoritative, is the schismatical temper, from which Cyprian was then most free when Stephen's intolerance put most pressure upon him to make rejoinder by counter-intolerance. Yet, "being most largely endowed with the holy bowels of Christian charity, he thought we ought to remain in Christian unity with those who differed from ourselves" in a matter lacking in ecumenical authority.

It has been to the absence of a similar temper in East and West that the Great Schism was due. We make a grievous mistake if we suppose that it was the result of any single fact—like the claim of Rome or the *Filioque* clause: it was in fact nothing less than the issue of a long drawn-out tendency to divergence in the Eastern and Western Churches, manifesting itself at Constantinople, at Chalcedon, in the preliminary division on the Monophysite controversy, till finally, after long ages, it took effect in the final separation. That there was much of the schismatical temper in the Roman Church, who can deny? The temper which will not tolerate differences which interfere with that uniformity of outward government which it loves: which is impatient of resistance to its designs: which sacrifices the claims of historical truth, and mercy, and love, to the

---

[1] See Augustin *de Bapt.* ii. 3-6, v. 25. He is following Jerome, who praises Cyprian on the same ground—that he did not anathematize those who differed from him (*adv. Lucif.* 25).

supremacy of a single see—this temper of intolerance and self-aggrandizement who can read history and deny to have been a governing element in the policy of the Roman Church even when controlled by so great a pontiff as Leo the First? Yet it is the temper of schism; it is responsible, in part, for the divisions it may create by retaliation and antagonism. It is human sin marring the divine witness to the unity of the Church's life. It fostered the spirit of antagonism in the Eastern Church—the blank conservatism which made 'mountains of molehills'; and held a novelty of custom in the rival Church as bad as an innovation upon authoritative doctrine; it fostered the counter-ambition which centred around the see of Constantinople; these again are marks of the temper of schism from which no part of the Church has in fact been free. The Great Schism took place. It destroyed neither part of the Church, but it reduced the fulness of corporate grace and life in both. Who shall divide the sin? No one but the great Judge. But we may be sure the schism will be perpetual, unless God's wonder-working power shall obliterate the temper of ambition and self-assertion in East and West, and granting to both the spirit of toleration in unessential differences, shall lead them again to be at one on the basis of agreement only in the common faith which has been the Church's heritage from the first.

Again, the temper of schism produced the separation of the Anglican Church from the rest of the West. In the Roman Church the temper of schism lay in the making a claim upon us so far greater than the universal consent of the Church could warrant. But who can deny that the schismatic spirit was at work in the Reformation in England? How much of impatient intolerance was there in the reforming spirit! How carelessly it denounced! How heedlessly it squandered priceless blessings in view of temporary or not irremediable evils! How unwilling it was to admit any fault in itself! We must admit as much as can be claimed of provocation to the spirit of reform in the condition of the Church, we must admit how impossible it seems for a reformation ever to be conducted in a moderate spirit—this is only to admit that human sin is not without palliation, without excuse; it does not amount to acquittal or approval.

And so with something of the schismatical temper, which is indeed nothing but the carnal temper of the old Adam, working in all parts of the Church, the holy bride of Christ on earth has reached her present divided and weakened condition. There is no catholic principle which can justify us in supposing that either the Roman, the Eastern, or the Anglican Church has been guilty of the sin of schism, in that sense in which schism is the act of self-withdrawal from the Church catholic. The English Church at the Reformation claimed to reform herself, and there is no catholic principle which forbade her to do it. She did not withdraw herself in so doing from the catholic Faith or the catholic Church; indeed she professed her intention to remain as fully in submission to the Church as before.

On this point indeed something remains to be said. For the present it is only intended to offer a brief and summary reply to the Roman claim that we are *ipso facto* schismatic in being separated from Rome. To this claim we Anglicans may reply:

1. There is no such thing as an absolute authority in any part of the Church. The authority of a pope is not even on his own showing greater than that of an apostle, yet at the last resort St. Paul conceives of an appeal behind even his own apostolic authority. "Though we, or an angel from heaven preach unto you any other gospel than that which we preached unto you, let him be anathema." Were then the authority of the papacy in Catholic tradition never so much greater than in fact it is, its authority could never be absolute, without appeal beyond it, unless it was indeed strictly infallible. But we are certain of nothing more than that truth shall never fail in the Church as a whole.

2. The authority of the papacy was as a fact the result of her ecclesiastical and spiritual merits, and of the requirements of circumstance. Catholic history throws us back at the last resort on Cyprian's principle of the independence of each episcopate, or at least on Augustin's, of the subordination of each only to the whole as represented in a general council. All gradations among bishops are of the *bene esse* of the Church, not of her *esse*. "There is no evidence of any divinely appointed order among the bishops."[1] And of course, further than this, whatever claim Rome might have made as the Head of a united Christendom is enormously weakened in force by the existence of millions of the Oriental Church separated from her communion, largely,

[1] *Roman Question* p. 9.

THE NATURE OF SCHISM.

perhaps we should say mainly, on account of the exaggeration of her claim to empire over other churches.

3. If it be urged that at least the ancient Church knew no *permanent* breaches of communion within her body and did not contemplate such as possible, we recognize the force of the objection. The fathers knew at least no breaches of communion as complete and permanent as we experience; they did not—St. Augustin for example did not—even contemplate the possibility of the Church permanently losing the fellowship of intercourse and love.[1] We can only reply by pointing out that St. Augustin was not a prophet of the future. He seems equally unable to contemplate the Church of Christ perishing in any part of the world where she had once been founded, so as to require restoration or refounding from some other part. The Mohammedan conquests and the permanent separations in the Church have in both respects falsified his anticipations. To no man is it given exactly to anticipate either the sorrows or the consolations of a future age. St. Athanasius—to give another instance of this—would have been shocked beyond measure if any one had told him that war would still be a feature in the national life of Christendom.[2]

But though all this argument be true, it is not the less

[1] See *de unitate Eccl.* There is however a remarkable chapter on the division of Judah and Israel (§ 33). Moreover there is nothing in the treatise about Rome as the centre of unity. On the indestructibility of the Church in any place where it has been planted see § 45.

[2] See *de Incarn.* 51, 52: he makes it one proof of Christ's Divinity that Greeks and barbarians, even the most savage races, when they become Christian, cease to make war.

the case that the emphasis which the fathers lay on the outward fellowship of the universal Church ought to make us lay to heart 'the great dangers we are in through our unhappy divisions.' At least there is the duty of acutely deploring the evil and praying for its remedy. It should never be forgotten that the saints in Jerusalem upon whose forehead was stamped the mark of the divine approval, were not those who had successfully countcracted, but those who felt and groaned over the evils under which God's people suffered.[1] And we have the further duty of guarding in our own Church against the schismatical temper. We must be rid of the intolerance which makes an authoritative claim upon the belief of others for matters which fall short of ecumenical consent. We must cultivate the faculty of distinguishing between authoritative doctrine and pious opinion, so that we may not stretch the meaning of heresy and put unnecessary obstacles in the way of internal reunion. And in the wider sphere it is of the greatest importance that we should grasp the breadth of our heritage, that we should realize the spirit of the creed in which we profess our belief, not in the Anglican, but in 'One Holy Catholic Church'; and if it would not be lawful for us, as indeed it would not, for the sake of external peace, to trample under foot conscience and history, and submit to whatever claim Rome may make upon us, it is not less our duty to endeavour to purge our own Church from the evils and unfaithfulnesses which have too often made the character and nature of our true mother hard to recognize.

[1] Ezek. ix. 4.

CHAPTER IX.

ANGLICAN ORDINATIONS.

EVERY Church which claims her fellowship in the catholic fraternity must be prepared not only to show that she is not wilfully schismatical, but also, and before that, to meet two legitimate challenges—to vindicate her orthodoxy, and to vindicate her orders, that is, her claim to be within the historical succession of the Church's life. "Let them produce," says Tertullian, "the account of the origins of their Churches; let them unroll the line of their bishops."[1] It is to meet this latter challenge in the case of the Anglican Church that we are now to apply ourselves.

First, however, let us clear the ground of certain subsidiary issues.

We set aside the question whether Rome has ever acknowledged or half acknowledged the validity of our orders. Our appeal all through has been behind Rome to the Church Catholic and it shall be so still. If our episcopate is questioned, so was St. Paul's apostolate, and we need not be more ashamed to defend ourselves than he was.

Once more let us assume now that our present orders are derived through Matthew Parker, conse-

[1] *Praescr.* 32.

crated Archbishop of Canterbury in 1559, so that their validity depends on the question whether he was a true bishop: in other words let us dismiss the question whether, if we had lost valid orders, we should not have recovered them in the consecration of Laud and Williams, in whom converged the three lines of the Italian, the Irish, and the English succession. This question [1] we dismiss simply because we really do not need any secondary supports.

I. Was then Matthew Parker validly consecrated? "Validly consecrated!" cried the Roman controversialist of old, "why, in place of consecration there was a sacrilegious scene in a tavern, when Scory, an apostate monk, struck the Queen's nominees on the head with a Bible, and bade them receive power to preach the word of God."[2] This "Nag's Head" fable was an impudent assertion of the Romanists at the beginning of the seventeenth century. Its utter baselessness is now admitted on all hands. We quote Canon Estcourt—the author of by far the ablest and most scientific modern Roman work adverse to our orders.[3] "It is very unfortunate that the Nag's Head story was ever seriously put forward; for it is so absurd on the face of it that it has led to the suspicion of Catholic theologians not being sincere in the objections they make to Anglican orders."

---

[1] Argued in *Priest's Prayer Book* "Anglican Orders" p. 204.

[2] Courayer *Anglican Ordinations* p. 92. We have not given the legend in full. Among other absurdities it implies that Scory was not himself a Bishop.

[3] *The Question of Anglican Ordinations* p. 154.

II. That Parker was consecrated, as is recorded in the Lambeth register, it is, as Canon Estcourt says, impossible to doubt: "It is impossible to doubt that everything did take place that is recorded in the Register."[1] The ceremony took place "about five or six o'clock in the morning." William Barlow, formerly, *i.e.* before Mary's accession, bishop of Bath and Wells, now elect of Chichester, John Scory, formerly bishop of Chichester, now elect of Hereford, Miles Coverdale, formerly bishop of Exeter, and John Hodgkins, bishop suffragan of Bedford, vested, the first "in a silk cope for the performance of the sacred rites," with his two chaplains similarly vested, the second and last in "linen surplices," the third, Coverdale, "only in a long woollen gown," "after prayers and suffrages . . . laid their hands on the archbishop and said in English, *viz.*, Take the Holy Ghost, and remember that thou stir up the grace of God, which is in thee by imposition of hands, etc. When this had been said, they gave the holy Bible into his hands, etc. After they had said this, the bishop of Chichester goes on to the remaining solemnities of the Communion, giving the archbishop no pastoral staff, with whom communicated the archbishop and the four other bishops mentioned above, with others beside." The historical truth of this account is now admitted. "But there is insufficient evidence" so runs the second plea "of Barlow himself having been consecrated." It would not be a matter of the first importance if this *were* doubtful, for all the consecrating bishops laid on their

[1] Pp. 96, 114. There is moreover a convergence of contemporary evidence. *Priest's Prayer Book* p. 205.

hands and *all repeated the words*.[1] Each bishop, therefore, performed the complete act of consecration, and the non-episcopal character of one of them would not affect the matter. But in fact there is no valid ground at all for doubting the fact of Barlow's consecration. The record of his actual consecration is indeed absent from the Lambeth Register,[2] but that is confessedly incomplete: 'The absence of any record of consecration,' says our opponent Mr. Hutton, 'would carry little weight.[3] On the other hand the supposition that he was not consecrated involves the most absurd consequences. It involves that a man, nominated bishop under Henry VIII. (A.D. 1536) who was always emphatic in his desire to minimize the doctrinal and ritual changes effected by the Reformation,[4] could by a

---

[1] This was a departure from the rubric of 1552. Probably they were only following the rubric of the Exeter Pontifical. That the assisting bishops are co-consecrators when they do *not* recite the words is certainly the more probable opinion. But when they all recite the words as well as lay on hands, there is surely no room for doubt. Yet that certainly occurred in this case, as Canon Estcourt admits p. 109. On this subject, and on the whole subject of Anglican Orders, let me refer to Mr. Brightman's admirable paper, *What Objections have been made to Anglican Orders* (S.P.C.K., for the 'Church Historical Society'). [I may add that the supposition of the Register not representing simply the original account of the Consecration has no bearing, as Escourt admits, on any of the matters stated above. We have the evidence of the Foxe MS. and the MS. in C.C.C. Cambridge.]

[2] His confirmation is recorded. The Diocesan Registers of St. David's and St. Asaph's, whence the omission might have been supplied, are lost.

[3] Hutton's *Anglican Ministry* p. 305. I formerly stated that 'the record of Bishop Gardiner's consecration is equally wanting.' But it exists, as the Dean of Winchester informs me, in the Register of that See. Day's case at Chichester is, however, analogous.

[4] It is ludicrous in discussing this possibility to omit to consider

mere whim refuse to be consecrated, and get the archbishop and bishops who ought to have consecrated him to omit the ceremony, thereby subjecting themselves to the pains and penalties of the statute of *praemunire*, and this in the days before the pontifical was reformed, whereas that same archbishop Cranmer, under the extreme reformer Edward VI., forced Hooper to submit to consecration, though he openly protested against the ceremony. It involves that he could sit, unchallenged, among bishops hostile to the Reformation in Convocation and the House of Lords—that he could get himself installed at St. David's and could carry through a long dispute with his chapter in which they left no stone unturned to dispute his rights to the privileges of the see. It involves lastly that he could be recognized as bishop by the bishops who repudiated the Reformation, Lee, Stokesley, Gardiner, and be officially recognized as bishop of Bath and Wells on Mary's accession, when he resigned his see—it involves that he could do all this without its ever being detected that he had not been consecrated at all.[1] Indeed the first men to doubt it

this *conservative* character of the king—in all respects opposed to the extreme Reformation party. Estcourt (p. 76) quite overlooks it. See Dr. Stubbs' *Lectures on Mediæval and Modern History*, p. 259: Henry "never forgot that he was the defender of the faith; nor, whatever were his eccentricities and aberrations in minor particulars, does he seem ever to have gone in this region further in the direction of change than the more enlightened popes and cardinals of his own age would have gone" . . . "doctrinally, although quite able to maintain his own line, he clearly symbolized consistently with Gardiner and not with Cranmer."

[1] For details of these undoubted facts consult Estcourt, esp. p. 78; Bailey's *Defence of English Orders*, especially on the dispute with the Chapter; and Hutton p. 313.

were men who lived eighty years after his consecration, and men of the class who invented and circulated the Nag's Head story. For it must always be remembered that when the imprisoned bishop Bonner in 1563 refused to take the oath of supremacy at the bidding of Horne, bishop of Winchester, in whose diocese his prison was situated, on the ground that Horne was "not elected, consecrated, and provided, according to laws of the Catholic Church, and the statutes and ordinances of this realm"—and that partly because his consecrator Parker was no true archbishop, his objection to Parker consisted (as explained by Coke) in the plea that his consecrators 'being bishops in the reign of Edward VI. were deprived in the reign of Queen Mary and were not restored before their presence at the consecration' —it was an objection, that is, to their legal status, not to their episcopal character.[1]

It is acknowledged [2] that there is no difficulty in assigning *a* date for Barlow's consecration. The fact indeed is one which can be challenged only in that spirit of criticism which can dissolve the evidence for Christ's Resurrection [3] and which has been parodied in the memorable "Historic Doubts about Napoleon Bonaparte" of Archbishop Whately.

---

[1] See Coke *Institutes* Ed. 1648 Part iii. c. 2 p. 34, Part iv. c. 17 pp. 321 f.; cf. Estcourt l.c. p. 108, 118, and Bramhall *Works* iii. 79.

[2] Estcourt p. 67. The difficulty is about *the* **date.**

[3] It is indeed a matter more for profound regret, than for surprise, that Mr. Hutton, of the Oratory, who objected some years ago to the evidence for Anglican orders, found himself shortly afterwards unable to accept the evidence for the Christian Religion.

ANGLICAN ORDINATIONS.

If it be urged that Barlow himself expressed contempt for his own orders, we reply that Barlow's own irreverence is admitted, but is at this stage of the argument nothing to the point: but Barlow's words when he said that "if the king's grace, being supreme head of the Church of England did nominate, choose, elect, any layman, being learned, to be a bishop, he so chosen, without mention made of any orders, *would be as good a bishop as he (Barlow) was, or the best in England"*— his words imply, as much as words could imply it, that Barlow had himself been duly consecrated. Indeed it is only pretended that he retained his position by a deliberate fraud, which would have exposed him to the greatest possible risks, for no assignable object in the world! "It is a mystery" Canon Estcourt admits "how he could have remained unconsecrated, or how he could have carried on his assumed character unchallenged, especially as he was involved in disputes with his Chapter."[1] But why should he have gone out of his way to remain unconsecrated, and on what possible ground of reason in the absence of all positive evidence to the effect can we be asked to believe he did?

We may sum up this discussion by quoting two opinions—the first that of the Roman Catholic historian Lingard: "When we find Barlow during ten years, the remainder of Henry's reign, constantly associated, as a brother, with the other consecrated bishops, discharging with them all the duties, both spiritual and secular, of a consecrated bishop, summoned equally with them to parliament and convocation, taking his seat among

[1] P. 81.

148   ANGLICAN ORDINATIONS.

them, according to seniority, and voting on all subjects as one of them; it seems most unreasonable to suppose, without direct proof, that he had never received that sacred rite, without which, according to the laws of both Church and State, he could not have become a member of the episcopal body."[1] The second shall be the opinion of Dr. Döllinger expressed so emphatically at the Bonn Reunion Conference[2]: "The result of my investigation is that I have no manner of doubt as to the validity of the episcopal succession in the English Church."[3]

In fact our opponents betray a consciousness of our secure historical position by their anxiety to do what they describe as "elevating the controversy to a higher ground."[4] Indeed that the real basis of their objection is not historical is evidenced by the fact that they show no greater disposition to accept the succession of the Anglican Church in Ireland than that in England.[5]

[1] *History of England* vi. p. 329 [note DD].

[2] *Bonn Conference* 1874 p. 51.

[3] The suspicions supposed to be justified by the peculiarities in the form of the grant of temporalities to Barlow (Estcourt p. 72) are dissolved by the discovery of an identical form of grant in the undisputed case of R. Ferrar (Rymer's *Fœdera*, London, 1713, vol. xv. 173 : "durante sua vita naturali"). The "suspicious circumstance" again of his being called "bishop" before consecration, when he was only bishop-elect, is now admitted to have many parallels and to have no "suspicions" attaching to it (Hutton *Anglican Ministry* p. 313).

[4] This is Dr. Newman's expression in a preface to Mr. Hutton's Book—surely very unworthy of its great author: cf. Hutton pp. 95, 304, 305.

[5] *Church Quarterly* vol. x. April 1880 p. 222.

III. But perhaps the Anglican form of ordination does not satisfy the requirements of the catholic Church. 'Of course it does not:' said the Roman controversialist of the seventeenth century. 'The essence of valid ordination—the necessary matter and form—is the delivery to the priest of the chalice and paten with the words: "Receive the power to offer sacrifice" etc. The Anglican ordinal is by this single omission rendered null and void. They have no priests and therefore no bishops.' So they spoke in great certainty, for indeed had not a pope in a solemn definition of faith announced this very doctrine about the 'sacrament of order' to the Armenians at the time of the Council of Florence? But alas for so satisfactory and conclusive an objection! it emerged through the historical studies of the great Roman theologian Morinus in the latter part of the seventeenth century, that this ceremony—this 'porrectio instrumentorum'—had been unknown in the Church for a thousand years, and the objectors had the double mortification of having the ground of their objection cut from under their feet, and of finding that the authoritative Roman theology had been elevating a ceremony of late introduction into the position of the 'essential matter and form' of orders, and degrading the true essential—the laying on of hands—into a subordinate and non-essential accompaniment. At any rate we hear no more of this confident objection.[1]

'But if the laying on of hands is sufficient matter,

[1] See *The Church and the Ministry* p. 68 note [1]; Estcourt pp. 261, 171, and Appendix 1.

the words "Receive the Holy Ghost," without specification[1] of the office of bishop or priest, are not sufficient form.' ('Form' it may be explained means the formula or words essential to the validity of a sacrament.) This was the last stronghold of objection against the regularity of the externals of Anglican ordination; and it is unnecessary that we should follow Anglican writers in arguing upon it, for Canon Estcourt has himself produced a decision of the Roman Church authoritative and emphatic, in the case of the Church of Abyssinia, which crushes this objection. We simply quote Canon Estcourt's pages.

"'Resolution of the Sacred Congregation of the Holy Office, given on Fer. iv., being the 9th of April 1704.—In Ethiopia, as it is necessary that the persons to be ordained should assemble for their ordination from distant parts at the city where the schismatic archbishop resides, and as he will only hold an ordination when persons to receive orders are collected together to the number of eight or ten thousand in the said city, he has therefore at such a time to ordain three or four thousand, or even more, in one day. In short, when those that are to receive the priesthood are arranged in ranks in the church, the archbishop passing hastily in front of them, imposes his hands on the head of each, saying *Accipe Spiritum Sanctum*. And for those to be ordained deacons he simply imposes the patriarchal cross on the head of each. And in consequence of the great multitude and the confusion and

---

[1] These specifications were introduced later into the Anglican Ordinations—in 1662.

the haste with which he proceeds, it follows that the archbishop on some does not impose his hands at all; and in other cases does not pronounce the words of the form; and not a few even are passed over without either one or the other. Hence the question is asked, whether priests and deacons in such a mode and form are validly ordained; and consequently whether such a priest on becoming a catholic ought to be admitted to the exercise of his orders; and by what rule in such circumstances ought a missionary to be guided?

'Resolution of the S.C. The ordination of a priest with imposition of hands and pronouncement of the form as stated in the case is valid; but the ordination of a deacon simply with imposition of the patriarchal cross is altogether invalid. Hence in admitting presbyters and deacons to the exercise of their orders after they have received the catholic faith, the following rules are to be observed:

'If a priest should say absolutely, that he was ordained with imposition of hands and pronouncement of the form, and if there should be no other impediment, the missionary, after giving him a dispensation from irregularity, and absolution from excommunication, may admit him to the exercise of his orders according to the rite, approved and expurgated, in which he was ordained.

'But if such a priest should ingenuously acknowledge that he has not a clear remembrance about the matter and form of his ordination, or if he has a doubt concerning either one or the other, he cannot be admitted to the exercise of his orders, till he has been ordained conditionally. And if he should absolutely assert that the imposition of hands and pronouncement of the form had been omitted, or either of them, he must be re-ordained absolutely, before he can be admitted to the exercise of his orders.

'But since it may happen that a person may have been validly ordained priest, though his ordination as deacon was invalid; in such a case, before he can exercise his orders, he ought, if it please the Sovereign Pontiff to grant faculties to the missionaries for that purpose, to receive a dispensation from irregularity, not only as having been ordained *per saltum*, but also as under suspension on account of the subsequent exercise of sacred orders,—at least for the time, until he can be validly promoted to the diaconate by a catholic bishop.'

"Such is this most important decision. And it will be seen at once that nothing could be more favourable to the Anglican side of the question. For it establishes the principle that the words *Accipe Spiritum Sanctum* are sufficient as a form of ordination to the priesthood; it renders nugatory the argument raised by Talbot and Lewgar, that the distinctive order must be named in the form; it makes it clear that, even if the Anglican form of the diaconate is invalid, this need not prevent the priesthood being validly conferred; it removes any doubt whether the uncanonical mode of altering the Anglican form would of itself have made it invalid; and it puts aside, as irrelevant, any questions whether the alteration was made by the Church or by the secular power; for no one can trace the origin of the use of this form among the Abyssinians [it is not to be found in their books], or find any authority for it beyond a mere custom that has crept in without any record of its introduction.

"The decision, indeed, refers only to the priesthood. But in the face of such an indication of the mind of the Church, it would be unbecoming to raise the question whether those same words, *Accipe Spiritum Sanctum*, are insufficient as a form for the episcopate also."[1]

IV. It remains then as an admission even of our adversaries that the Anglican form of ordination is in itself valid. What then can hinder its acceptance in our case? Something not outward but inward; the argument is again taken on to 'higher ground'—even into the cloud-land of 'intention,' or else our opponents are constrained to make their appeal to *a priori* considerations of a very dangerous character. Thus Mr. Hutton, whose work we have alluded to above as having received the sanction of a preface from Cardinal Newman, appeals to the 'moral evidence against the reality of the Anglican priesthood'—or again the '*prima facie* evidence' 'whose persuasiveness is greater than that of any bare arguments.' The Anglican Church in history has not, Mr. Hutton and Cardinal Newman think, *looked* as if it had a priesthood. It is almost charitable to suppose it has not had it. As if one were to argue from the unworthy lives of Christians to the conclusion that they had not received the Baptismal grace. Has the average

[1] Pp. 190-192. The decision of the S. C. given above was confirmed in 1860. But see Appended Note v. p. 214.

life of Christians been such as to make this method of argument a secure one? Assuredly not; it has been such as to make it a constant pretext for schism. The true method of argument for a Catholic is to appeal to outward sacramental transactions in history, and rest assured that the outward transaction is the pledge of the inward grace, and that what is needed is not to doubt the adequacy of the formal transaction, but to stir up the inward grace. The Church of England is stirring up the inward grace of her priesthood. We are not arguing how much cause she may have to be ashamed of her past use of it. But we would vigorously maintain that all the security of the sacramental system is gone if we may argue from a general neglect of a gift to its non-existence. That 'the tree is known by its fruits' is a great truth. It means that holiness can only proceed from the Holy Spirit, and that you can argue back from the effect to the cause. But it does not mean that there can be no such thing in the Christian Church—whether Oriental, Roman, or Anglican—as a talent hid away in a napkin, a light kept under a bushel.

And now what is the doctrine of defective intention which is to invalidate Anglican orders? That 'the unworthiness of the minister hinders not the grace of the sacraments,' is a great principle to which the Roman Church at least is thoroughly committed. Where you have the external conditions of validity for a sacrament, a right 'form' and 'matter' and 'minister'—to use the technical terms already explained—there no spiritual disqualification, whether in understanding or morals, on the part of the administrator, is a bar to the validity of the rite, and this because of the great principle that the giver of the grace is not the minister, but the Holy Spirit. This principle in regard to the validity of baptism and ordinations administered by heretics or schismatics was fought out by St. Augustin against the Donatists. We assume it now and ask only—for what sort of doctrine of 'requisite intention' does this leave room? For no more than that which Hooker asserts. "Furthermore" he says, "because definitions are to express but the most immediate and nearest parts of nature, whereas other principles farther off, although not specified in defining, are notwithstanding in nature implied and presupposed, we must note that inasmuch as sacraments are actions religious and mystical, which nature they have not unless they proceed *from a serious meaning;* and what every man's private mind is, as we cannot know, so neither are we bound to examine; therefore always in these cases the known intent of the Church generally doth suffice, and where the contrary is not manifest, we may presume that he which outwardly doth the work, hath inwardly the purpose of the Church of God."

If the requirement of intention reaches beyond this point, it becomes as Jewel calls it "the very dungeon of uncertainty." "The heart of man is unsearchable; if we stay upon the intention of a mortal man, we may stand in doubt of our own baptism." Even within this narrow limit we must recollect that the old story of the baptism by the boy Athanasius shows that the churchmen of the early days could regard as valid a baptism administered in play.[1] But we may assent freely to Hooker's requirement of intention. We need it, to guard against the possibility of sacraments being consecrated by accident, through a chance collocation of words and materials. This much, then, is granted and no more. In applying this principle to the present controversy, we base our contention on the statement of it given by Canon Estcourt.[2]

"The intention requisite for the valid administration of a sacrament is the *intentio generalis faciendi quod facit ecclesia*. Hence a sacrament conferred with the correct matter and form by a heretic, or even an atheist, is valid, if he intends to do that rite which the Church does,—and not specially the Roman Church, but the Church *in confuso;* even though he might not believe in the reality of the sacrament. And supposing the form be clear and genuine, and the sense of the words is preserved in its integrity, even if the form were changed with an erroneous or heretical intent, the

[1] The evidence for this depends, not on the truth of the story, but on its prevalence, as against Hutton, p. 179.

[2] P. 199 cf. Card. Newman *Via Media* vol. i. p. 339. "In like manner even though a bishop were to use the words, 'receive ye the Holy Ghost,' with little or no meaning, or a priest the consecrating words in the Eucharist, considering it only a commemoration of Christ's death, or a deacon the water and the words in baptism, denying in his heart that it is regeneration; yet they may in spite of their unbelief, be instruments of a power they know not of; and 'speak not of themselves.'" To this is appended in the last edition (1877) the note "Certainly, if the power has been given them." Of course the Roman Church must grant the validity of orders conferred by unbelievers, to meet, for example, such a case as that of Prince Talleyrand, bishop of Autun, and no doubt many other cases in the Middle Ages and at the time of the Italian Renaissance.

sacrament would still be valid. For no amount of heretical intention would invalidate it, provided that he intended in a general way to do what the Church does, and that he does not overthrow or destroy the legitimate sense of the words."

Well now, had the English Church of the Reformation period—not any individual bishop, but the English Church, as represented in the official utterances of her Ordination rite—had she this 'general intention of doing what the Church does,' not the Roman Church, but the Church 'in the vague'? Did she intend to continue the old orders of the Church, and did therefore every Anglican bishop (as officially representing the Church, not 'in his private mind') have the only sort of intention which can be possibly allowed to be requisite? It is surely sufficient answer to quote the language of the Preface to our services of ordination: "It is evident unto all men diligently reading the Holy Scripture and ancient authors, that from the Apostles' time there have been these orders of ministers in Christ's Church — Bishops, Priests, and Deacons. Which offices were evermore had in such reverent estimation that no man might presume to execute any of them, except he were first called, tried, examined . . . and also by public prayer, with imposition of hands, were approved and admitted thereunto by lawful authority. And therefore, to the intent that these orders may be continued, and reverently used and esteemed in the Church of England, etc." '*To the intent that these orders may be continued*'!—there is, then, we contend, no further ground of argument on this score. The English Church had a serious mind to continue the old orders in the Reformed Church; for their continuance she provided a proper minister, and proper rite, valid in 'matter and form.' What further ground of attack is there? Mr. Hutton falls back on a doctrine of the private intention of the celebrant of a sacrament which would make all orders precarious—nay, all sacraments.[1] We say with St. Thomas Aquinas [2]: "The minister of a sacrament acts as the representative (in persona) of the whole Church of which he is the minister; in the words which he utters, the *intention of the Church is expressed*, which suffices to the perfection of a sacrament, unless the contrary be expressed outwardly on the part of the minister, or recipient of the sacrament."

Canon Estcourt falls back rather on a doctrine which is both wanting in catholic authority and surely tends to militate against the true principle of sacramental grace. The Church (it is maintained) only confers by her sacraments what she intends to confer.

[1] Pp. 179, 327.
[2] *Summa*, pars iii. q. lxiv. art. 8. Of course a later school of Roman theologians would not admit this doctrine. But we are not concerned to maintain that no school of theologians, on any principle they may devise, can object to Anglican orders, but only that they cannot be objected to on grounds which can be called catholic. How insecure an extreme requirement of inward intention may make all orders is shown by Mr. Hutton's own statement, p. 523:—

"Accepting as we do the position that the succession is continued through single lines and not by way of threefold interlacing cords, we have to maintain that each bishop in the chain which historically connects, say Cardinal Manning with the Apostles, was validly baptized, validly ordained to the priesthood, and

If the mind of the Anglican Church can be shown to be deficient on the doctrine of the priesthood, it follows that she did not intend by her priesthood all that the catholic Church intends by it—therefore she did not convey to her ministers what lay outside her own conceptions.

To this our reply is twofold : so far as we are here dealing with an attack upon the orthodoxy of the English Church, we prefer to deal with the matter on its own ground. Whether a Church has orders and whether she is orthodox are *two* questions, not one.[1]

But so far as the doctrine is asserted that the grace given by a sacrament depends on the mind of the particular part of the Church in which it is administered, we entirely decline to accept the doctrine. We believe[2]

validly consecrated to the episcopate. . . . It must be allowed that this position is, humanly speaking, indefensible. But Catholics are, nevertheless, absolutely certain that they have the true ministerial succession, inasmuch as it is as indefectible as is the Church herself. '

And in a note :—

"Catholics, of course, are not called upon to hold that in no single case has there been a bishop who for lack of valid baptism, ordination, or consecration, was a bishop only in name. But they may well believe that the government of the Church would be so providentially ordered as to hinder such a person from being called on to continue the succession. It falls to the lot of comparatively few bishops to act as the principal consecrator of others."

[1] Canon Estcourt argues in a manner unworthy of him in his miserable Chapter vi. in which he tries to explain away the language of the English office for the Ordination of Priests. Has he read Hooker Bk. v. cap. lxxvii. ? Hooker gives to the Anglican office a meaning than which it cannot carry a lower.

[2] This is supported by a recent decree of the Roman Inquisition (1872) cited in Puller, *The Bull Apostolicae Curae*, S.P.C.K. 1896, p. 57 f.

that a baptism administered in due form by Baptists, is valid, in spite of their heretical mind, formally expressed, on baptism. The grace of a sacrament depends not on the mind of any particular part of the Church, but on the intention of the Holy Ghost which can find expression only in the catholic doctrine of the whole Church. We are ready enough to vindicate the orthodoxy of the Anglican Church. But had she denied *in toto* the sacrificial aspect of the Eucharist, as she has assuredly not done, her denial would have affected her position in orthodoxy, not her orders.[1] The grace of orders depends on the original intention and will of the Holy Ghost, and all that we do is to hand on the gift by a sacramental method. The method is intrusted to us; the gift is given by Him: and our insufficient conception of it does in no wise impair its fulness. St. Augustin's language on this subject is quite explicit. "Accordingly[2] if Marcion consecrated the sacrament of Baptism with the words of the Gospel 'in the name of the Father and of the Son and of the Holy Ghost,' the sacrament was complete, though his faith was not complete, but stained with error. . . . If sacraments are the same they are everywhere complete, even when they are wrongly understood." "If a man[3] offers an erroneous prayer (in baptism) God is present to uphold the words of His gospel, without which the baptism of Christ cannot be consecrated, and He Himself consecrates His sacrament, that in the recipient who turns in truth to God either before he is baptized, when he is baptized, or at some future time, that very sacrament may be profit-

[1] On the argument of the Bull 'Apostolicae Curae,' see Chap. xi.
[2] *de Bapt.* iii. 15.   [3] vi. 25.

able to salvation, which were he not to be converted, would be powerful to his destruction. But who is there who does not know that there is no baptism of Christ, if the words of the gospel in which consists the outward visible sign be not forthcoming? But you will more easily find heretics who do not baptize at all, than any who baptize without those words. And therefore we say, not that every baptism (for in many of the blasphemous rites of idols men are said to be baptized), but that the baptism of Christ, that is, every baptism consecrated in the words of the Gospel, is everywhere the same, and cannot be vitiated by any perversity on the part of any men."

V. There is still one more charge to which we must reply. It is asserted that the English bishops, if they have valid orders, have no *jurisdiction*, and though this is in effect only the charge of schism revived in another form, it is necessary not to leave it unanswered.

Consecration we must explain conveys in one sense a universal mission, a share in Christ's universal commission to 'go and make disciples of all nations.' Each Apostle had, and each bishop has, in an abstract sense, this universal mission which carries with it, and indeed is not distinguishable from, what, in the technical language of theology, may be called 'habitual' jurisdiction.[1] But even amongst the Apostles the exercise of this jurisdiction was limited by mutual arrangement,[2] and in the early Church every bishop was limited to a

---

[1] See *Church Quarterly* vol. xi. Jan. 1881 : *Mission and Jurisdiction*, and Blunt's *Dict. of Hist. and Doct. Theol.*, Art. Jurisdiction.
[2] Gal. ii. 9, Rom. xv. 20, 2 Cor. x. 13-16.

proper diocese, in which alone he was allowed to exercise his functions. Within this sphere alone he has *actual jurisdiction*, i.e. the ecclesiastical right to exercise his functions. Actual jurisdiction is indeed to be regarded, not as a gift super-added to the gift of order, but as the right to exercise this gift within the limit determined by ecclesiastical arrangements from time to time. In Erastian epochs of the Church's life, as under the Byzantine emperors, under Frankish kings, or in periods of the English Church, the secular authority has had a predominant, or even practically exclusive, power over these arrangements, but however the limits of actual jurisdiction are settled, the jurisdiction itself is regarded (from the only point of view which can be called catholic) as inherent in the see. It is entered upon when any bishop is enthroned in his see in a canonical manner, and the idea of a bishop consecrated to no see was abhorrent to the Church's mind. That the pope is the sole source of jurisdiction, and that the Anglican bishops when they ceased to be recognized by the pope became *ipso facto* schismatic, is no doubt a claim of the papacy and a mediæval doctrine, but it has been made sufficiently plain in earlier chapters that it has no claim to be regarded as part of the Church's catholic heritage. It would indeed be nothing less than ludicrous to apply the idea at all to early church history.[1] Now I do not think that any one would really dream of

---

[1] "Readers of history hardly need to be told that the bishop of Rome was never asked to give either mission or jurisdiction to anybody for the first six centuries of the Christian era." *Church Quarterly* l.c. p. 403.

ANGLICAN ORDINATIONS. 163

questioning the jurisdiction of the Anglican episcopate except on the basis of the idea that the pope is the sole fount of jurisdiction, and as that position has been already dealt with—as it has been made quite plain that the whole Anglican position involves an appeal behind the papacy to the principles of the ancient and the universal Church—I cannot think this question of jurisdiction a very serious one. Church history presents us with innumerable irregularities in episcopal succession, but we are not allowed to go back upon them. I hope to show that the *technical* defence of Anglican jurisdiction is adequate, but if it were much less adequate than it is, the contention would still hold that the Anglican succession holds the ground legitimately by default. There was no rival claimant to the see of Canterbury. It is quite true that the atmosphere of the Tudor kingdom is not an atmosphere in which the free canonical action of the Church is likely to flourish, but the 'Erastian' authoritativeness of the Tudors is quite as prominent in Mary's reign as in Edward's or Elizabeth's, and no more destroys the possibility of jurisdiction in Anglican prelates, than in Byzantine or Frankish bishops of similar epochs.[1]

With this preface, we advance our technical defence, which must be based on a brief review of the ecclesiastical situation at the beginning of Elizabeth's reign.

The 'concession' of the clergy in 1531 which acknowledged his Majesty Henry VIII. "the sole pro-

---

[1] This paragraph I should wish to euphasize. On the subject of Erastianism see the excellent essay of Dean Church *On the Relations between Church and State* (London, Walter Smith) 1881.

tector of the Church and clergy of England, its unique and supreme lord, and, as far as Christ's law allows, even its supreme head," had been passed without any dissent in the convocation of Canterbury, and in the convocation of York with no more than Tunstal's protest on the ground that "though to most men the words seem without danger of any offence, yet some suspected of heresy . . . taking their sense perversely have endeavoured to escape the judgment of their bishops." Tunstal moreover accepted the headship subsequently, as well as an abjuration of the papal authority, when Parliament, in accordance with the resolution of convocation, required him, with the other bishops, to swear to it.[1] This resolution accords well with a petition commonly attributed to convocation,[2] that if the Pope should persist in demanding the payment of Annates "the obedience of the king and people be withdrawn" from the see of Rome, as in like case the French king "withdrew the obedience of him and his subjects" from Pope Benedict XIII.; and with the declaration of three years later, "the Pope had not any greater jurisdiction conferred upon him by God than any other foreign bishop."[3] Nothing was done in Mary's reign to reverse formally these synodical acts.

[1] See Mr. Gladstone's *Elizabethan Settlement of Religion* (*Nineteenth Cent.* July 1888) p. 7. The remainder of this chapter is largely based on this article.

[2] Wilkins' *Concilia* iii. 760, but legitimate doubt has been thrown upon its origin, and I desire to express no opinion; in *State Papers*, Henry VIII. v. p. 344, no. 722 (5) it is called a petition of Parliament.

[3] There was a similar resolution of the York convocation, Collier *Eccl. Hist.* iv. 263.

They were of course reversed, but only by Act of Parliament, and the same authority cancelled these reversals in the first year of Elizabeth. This certainly left it open to the Queen to act upon the unrepealed declarations of the convocation, all the more that the episcopal body which met with its composition unchanged at the beginning of Elizabeth's reign under her brief, took no steps at all, even at the solicitation of the lower house, to repudiate its earlier action.[1] When therefore a legal oath was required of the bishops, an oath "which asserted on the behalf of the Crown less than was contained in the unrepealed and still effective declaration of the Anglican convocations," there was nothing irregular in the requirement, and, considering the period at which it occurred, nothing violent in their deprivation for refusal to take it. It happened curiously enough that of the twenty-seven bishops alive at the Queen's accession, eleven died before she took action. Of the remaining sixteen, all but one—Kitchen of Landaff—refused the oath. They had withdrawn from the position which even Bishops of a conservative mind were not afraid in most cases to take up in Henry's reign. Their consequent deprivation was justified by the action of the Church and was in accordance with the law of the land.[2] It contrasted in this respect with the utterly unconstitutional way in which Mary, following Edward's precedent, had deprived a great number of bishops simply by royal commission, with no justification at all.

---

[1] Gladstone *l.c.* p. 11.
[2] They were deprived for refusal to take the oath, not for their previous refusal to consecrate Parker. Lingard vi. 8.

It should be noted further that four or five of the bishops deprived by Queen Elizabeth had died before any measures were taken to supply anew the episcopal bench, and of the remaining ten or eleven, at least four or five were disqualified altogether for appealing to their canonical rights, inasmuch as they had been most uncanonically introduced into their sees by Queen Mary in the lifetime of their proper occupants.[1]

Thus when Parker was consecrated it was by bishops as canonically 'provincial' as was possible under the circumstances. Coverdale, formerly bishop of Exeter, had been quite uncanonically deposed on Mary's accession, and only allowed to escape with his life beyond seas;[2] and Barlow had only resigned under pressure. Scory and Hodgkins were bishops within the province, who could be properly summoned to assist. The former indeed had held the see of Chichester,[3] and was now elect of Hereford, as Barlow was of Chichester. Thus, as the see of Canterbury was duly vacated by death: as Parker was elected by the chapter and confirmed without opposition in Bow Church: as he was consecrated by bishops of whom two or three could rightly be called provincial: as there was no official

[1] Palmer *On the Church* i. p. 486. He also points out that four or five others had been put into their sees by papal provisions contrary again to the mind of the English Church as represented in the declaration of convocation, twenty years before.

[2] I think, in spite of what Mr. Rivington says (*Dependence* p. 145), that Coverdale was a legitimate bishop. See Dixon *Hist. of the Church of England*, iii. p. 276, and the account of him in the *Dict. of Nat. Biography*. No doubt however 'Erastianism' colours all ecclesiastical proceedings at this period.

[3] He was intruded by Edward and dispossessed by Mary.

or formal protest at the time and no rival claimant to the see: as finally the formal withdrawal of the Romanist body from the jurisdiction of the Anglican episcopate did not take place for eleven years, and even then there was no establishment of a rival episcopate—we cannot see how any objection can be raised to the claim of Parker and his successors to sit in the seat of Augustin, and to inherit the jurisdiction which belongs to that see.

CHAPTER X.

ANGLICAN ORTHODOXY.

IF enough has already been said to vindicate the Church of England against the charge of wilful schism, and against such imputations upon the validity of her orders as would thrust her out of the Church's constitutional unity—yet a reply has still to be made on the charge of heresy.

What is heresy? It is the self-willed repudiation by an individual or a part of the Church of the authoritative rule of faith, especially as embodied in some ecumenical dogmatic decree. What the standard of faith is has been explained already at some considerable length. It remains to ask whether the English Church has rebelled against it.

The Reformation in England was not primarily a *doctrinal* movement at all. In its first intention it was a movement to repudiate papal usurpation, and good care was taken to emphasize the stability of the Anglican position as regards doctrine. "Our said sovereign the king and all his natural subjects, as well spiritual as temporal, continue to be as obedient, devout, catholic and humble children of God and holy Church as any people be within any realm christened."[1] Afterwards,

---

[1] *Stat.* 23 Henry VIII. c. 20. See Hardwick *Church History* Reformation p. 179.

the doctrinal movement became much more prominent, but the intention of the Anglican Church was never lost sight of—it was to repudiate abuses and later accretions and to retain the original and catholic doctrine. The convocation of 1571, which imposed on the clergy subscription to the Articles of Religion, issued a canon to preachers enjoining them to "teach nothing in their sermons which they should require to be devoutly held or believed by the people except what is agreeable to the doctrine of the Old and New Testaments, and what the ancient fathers and catholic bishops have collected out of that said doctrine." The "authority of the Church in controversies of faith" is maintained in the 20th Article, and the intention of the Anglican branch not "to forsake or reject the Churches of Italy, France, Spain and Germany" except in points where they were fallen from "their ancient integrity and from the Apostolical Churches," is asserted in the Canons.[1] So also the formal appeal of Anglican divines as a whole has been to the 'quod ubique, quod semper, quod ab omnibus' and to Scripture.

But, however good her abstract intention, may not the English Church in fact have been betrayed into some authoritative and formal repudiation of an integral part of the Catholic faith, during the wild confusion of the Reformation epoch? The question, we must observe, is as to formal and authoritative repudiation. There was a wild reaction against Mediævalism during the sixteenth century, and many of the extreme reformers in England and in Europe generally held views which

[1] No. 30, *The lawful use of the Cross in baptism explained*

we could not acquit of heresy, but we are not in any way committed to their views, except so far as they have affected our formularies.

There are two further remarks which we must make by way of preliminary. Persons whom it would be hard to call orthodox have been teachers in the Church of England in the sixteenth century and later, and we may be therefore quite sure that the standard of doctrinal discipline in the Church of England has been often unsatisfactory:—but there is a vital distinction between heresy and a failure of doctrinal discipline. We admit the charge of doctrinal laxity sorrowfully enough, but undiscipline does not unchurch a Church. A man may cry out with St. Basil: "Our tribulations are proclaimed the whole world over. The doctrines of the fathers are despised; the apostolic traditions are reckoned for nothing; the discoveries of innovating men hold sway in the Churches; men are no longer theologians but logical disputants. True shepherds are banished and grievous wolves are brought in."[1] Such a condition of things cannot be deplored too deeply, nor can we strive too earnestly after a remedy for it, but the evil is not that the Church's teaching is heretical, but that men are allowed to teach in her name what is not her doctrine.[2] This undiscipline in doctrine is at least no worse than undiscipline in morals. Tolerated teach-

[1] Ep. xc. : cf. Pref. p. xii.

[2] It is important, I think, to notice that people are often accused of heresy when they should only be accused of rash language. Mr. Rivington speaks as if there were a good deal of denial of everlasting punishment in the Church of England. It seems to me that a great many who use what seems very rash language, guard

ing of error[1] no more decatholicizes a Church than tolerated laxity of clerical morals, of which the history of the Churches of the Roman obedience affords only too many examples, extending over great epochs of time. No doubt the English Church largely sold her freedom to exercise her own discipline in payment for her position in the State, and the crippling of her disciplinary action is the penalty, the sore and humiliating penalty, for her undue confidence in the permanent Churchmanship of the national rulers. We attempt no sort of justification for the deplorable subordination to the State into which the English Church allowed herself to be betrayed, but Erastianism no more decatholicizes the doctrine of the English Church than it did that of the Byzantine Church of old or of the Frankish Church in the Middle Ages.

The other preliminary remark which must be made is this. There are in every age a number of misleading phrases justified by prescription but by nothing else, adopted simply because they save the trouble of thought and have a sort of authoritative sound which is the next best substitute for truth. Among such phrases is the 'Reformation settlement.' It requires very little knowledge to make us see that in no department of human action, political or social, intellectual or theological, was

themselves against denying it, *e.g.* notably Dr. Farrar : see *Mercy and Judgment* p. 1 : "I have never denied and do not now deny the possible endlessness of punishment." Cf. Pusey's letter to him, quoted by himself : *Guardian*, Oct. 10, 1888, p. 1503.

[1] 'No,' says F. Richardson (p. 145), 'the toleration of heresy is distinctly heretical.' How does this apply to Honorius? He is defended by Romanists as having only tolerated, not professed, the heresy of the Monothelites.

the Reformation age an age which admitted of 'settlement.' It was an age of awakening, an age of transition, but that is just the opposite of an age of settlement. As in every other department of life so it was in theology. The Roman theology of the Council of Trent represents no final settlement. It is theology at the half-way house between catholicity pure and simple, and Ultramontane Romanism. Has the history of the Calvinist and Lutheran Churches suggested the idea that their theology reached a 'settlement' in the days of their respective founders? As for the English Church, her theological *intention* was good, and she was mercifully spared the action upon her of any of those masterful individualities and uncatholic wills, which helped the foreign Reformations down different roads of heretical defection. But when we ask whether the English Church of the Reformation arrived at a satisfactory statement of doctrine in accordance with her fundamental intentions—at a permanent 'settlement'—we must, we fancy, answer to a great extent in the negative. She was in fact suffering from reaction, and her formulas are too often protests against what is exaggerated or false, rather than statements of what is true. She was more at pains to arrive at a working compromise than at a clear statement. Indeed she had not, the Church at large had not, a knowledge of ancient liturgies or ancient theology, such as would have admitted of a position being formulated which could be regarded as (from a simply catholic point of view) a satisfactory settlement.

When we have said this it becomes apparent that we do not think catholic-minded people can be in any

ANGLICAN ORTHODOXY. 173

idolatrous attitude towards the English Reformation, or indeed that we can take an optimistic view of the process. The ship of the Church went through a great storm—she lost a great deal, not only in decoration and accoutrements, but in rigging and in bulwarks, but she came out of that storm—the ship. So far then we can accept the statement of our case from Cardinal Newman's lips: "There was a very trying interval for the Church of England in the sixteenth century, when it ran great risk of being wrecked; but it weathered the storm, and its good fortune may be regarded as a providence and become a positive argument for its being what . . . its great history betokens."[1]

And now to enter more into detail—the Church of England is conspicuously orthodox on the great fundamentals of the Trinity and the Incarnation. She accepts —as an establishment no less than as a Church—the ecumenical Councils as criteria of heresy.[2] Nor is it merely that her Creeds and Articles are formally orthodox. It is true further that no Church can boast a richer, more eloquent, more learned, or more powerful body of theology, dogmatic and apologetic, than the post-Reformation Church of England can exhibit on these subjects, beginning with Richard Hooker and coming down to the present day.

But it may be urged that even the Incarnation is not rightly held unless it be held in its proper relation to us and our present lives—unless it be viewed in its 'extension' in the Church and through the sacraments.

[1] Pref. to Hutton's *Anglican Ministry* p. viii.
[2] *Stat.* 1 Elizabeth. See Hardwick p. 225.

Here, then, also, the orthodoxy of the English Church does not admit of a doubt. She plainly asserts that the sacraments are means of grace, are the means through which the grace of the new life of Christ is communicated to us. Her definition of sacraments in general as "effectual signs of grace" is simply the definition of the Roman schools. It asserts that the sacraments are symbols, and not only symbols—that they also effect or convey what they symbolize—they are 'practica' or 'efficacia signa gratiae.' This is undoubtedly the catholic doctrine, which as it is implied with reference to Baptism in the Nicene Creed, so it is further expounded with great clearness with reference to Baptism and the Eucharist in the later part of the Catechism.

Then with reference to the Holy Eucharist in particular the Church of England unmistakably teaches that the Body and Blood of Christ are therein given, taken and eaten, after a spiritual and heavenly manner —that (in Hooker's words) "Christ in the Sacrament imparteth Himself even in His whole entire Person unto every soul that receiveth Him." Further that "what merit, force, or virtue soever there is in His sacrificed Body and Blood, we freely, fully, and wholly have it by this Sacrament," for "here we receive Christ and those graces that flow from Him in that He is man," "and the effect thereof is a real transmutation of our souls and bodies from sin to righteousness, from death and corruption to immortality and life." This is beyond a doubt the positive and emphatic teaching of the Anglican Prayer-book, and it was not for no purpose that she brought back into emphasis the indirect but most real effect of the Holy Communion upon our *bodies*, a truth of which much had been made in the early Church. Beyond this if the formulas of the Church do not commit us to any definite view as to the nature of Christ's presence in the sacrament we must remember that there was no formulated dogma of Catholic authority on the subject, that the moment was by no means opportune for definition, and that very possibly no more exact determination of the doctrine than existed in the ancient Church is even desirable. At any rate the absence of it is not heretical.[1]

It is not however at all reasonable to dispute that there are defects in the teaching of the English formularies taken alone, and it is necessary to refer to them.

We do conceive that in her desire to restore the communion of the people to its proper prominence in the eucharistic office, and in her reaction from mediæval misconceptions, and abuses connected with the 'mass-

[1] See Keble's *Letters* cxviii-cxxi. It would appear that while the English Church (*a*) excludes a materialistic view of the Real Presence in the 'declaration on kneeling,' and the current view of transubstantiation, and (*b*) on the other side affirms a real communication of the Body and Blood of Christ in the sacrament, she may be said to leave the intermediate ground open. This is Bossuet's view of the matter and it can hardly be described as unfair. It must be remembered however that when the declaration on kneeling was reinstated in 1662, the words which condemned adoration in the sacrament of a 'real and essential presence there being of Christ's natural flesh and blood' were struck out (they had no more than the authority of an order of council in 1552 and had no existence in Elizabeth's Prayer-book) and the words 'corporal presence of Christ's natural flesh and blood' substituted. Thus the Church deliberately refused to condemn an adoration of Christ *really* present.

ing priests,' the Church of England unduly obscured and threw into the background the doctrine of the eucharistic sacrifice. She is not heretical. Her 31st Article is only intended to guard jealously the unique completeness of the sacrifice made by Christ upon the Cross—to guard it, moreover, not as against any formulated doctrine such as that of Trent, but as against a current popular view; and who that knows what has been 'commonly said' in mediæval and modern Roman theology, can doubt that it needs guarding?[1] For the

[1] A doctrine prevailed in the middle ages that while the sacrifice of the Cross was the satisfaction for original sin, the sacrifice of the Mass is the satisfaction for actual sin. This is asserted in sermons *de Sacramento Eucharistiae*, falsely ascribed to Albertus Magnus (see tom. xii. p. 250. Lyons, 1651): "Secunda causa institutionis huius sacramenti est sacrificium altaris, contra quandam quotidianam delictorum nostrorum rapinam. Ut sicut corpus Domini semel oblatum est in cruce pro debito originali; sic offeratur jugiter pro nostris quotidianis delictis in altari et habeat in hoc ecclesia munus ad placandum sibi Deum super omnia legis sacramenta vel sacrificia pretiosum et acceptum." That this doctrine was not only once stated, but became current and prevalent, is shown by the language of the confession of Augsburg pt. ii. art 3: "There was added the opinion which augmented private masses indefinitely, viz. that Christ satisfied by his passion for original sin and instituted the mass as an oblation for daily sins mortal and venial." A similar view is referred to by Latimer, *Sermon* iv. (ed. Parker Soc., vol. i. p. 36): "While they then preached to the people the redemption that cometh by Christ's death to serve only them that died before His coming, that went in the time of the Old Testament; and that now since, redemption and forgiveness of sins, purchased by money and devised by men, is of efficacy, and not redemption purchased by Christ." Such is the background of our 31st Article. It also has in view the undue separation of the priest from the Church, whose mouthpiece he is, in the sacrifice of the altar; cf. *The Church and the Ministry* p. 85.

A view has recently become prevalent, both popularly and in theology, in the Roman Church, which makes each Mass a sub-

ANGLICAN ORTHODOXY. 177

Eucharist is not even mystically a *renewal* of Christ's passion but an act of co-operation with Christ's heavenly intercession. Christ upon the eucharistic altar is only 'offered' in the sense that His once-made sacrifice is there perpetually presented and pleaded before the Father, as in heaven, so on earth. The altar is, so to speak, on a line not with Calvary, but with the heavenly Intercession.

Unfortunately however,—there being no authoritative dogma to force the compilers of our Prayer-book to positive statement—they contented themselves with an indefinite protest against current error and gave no positive teaching on the Eucharistic sacrifice. The force of the Protestant reaction was further allowed to rob the Anglican Eucharistic office of a great deal of quite primitive language. No doubt we retained the words from the pre-Reformation Mass about 'the Sacrifice of

stantive sacrifice, distinct from, though dependent upon, the sacrifice of the cross. Christ, it is contended by the recent Roman theologians, gives Himself afresh to be sacrificed in each Mass at the hands of the priest. Each Mass is a fresh 'self-emptying,' a fresh 'immolation,' a renewed 'reduction' of Christ to a state of humiliation. Without this it would not be a proper sacrifice. I have endeavoured elsewhere to give the theological statements of this lamentable doctrine, as found in De Lugo, or Franzelin (see a sermon on *The Eucharistic Sacrifice*, pub. by the C.B.S., 1889), and as an instance of its popular treatment, I would refer to Canon Gilbert's *Love of Jesus* Fifteenth Edition, with the *imprimatur* of Cardinal Manning pp. 41, 46: ' We hold that here [at the Altar] in a mystical manner Thy Body and Blood are separated, and that Thou art, as it were, again nailed to the Cross, and presented to Heaven as a holocaust, for the propitiation of the sins of the world. . . . Why was not one Atonement, dearest Lord, one Sacrifice, one Calvary sufficient ? . . . Thou knewest . . . that we should contemn Thy first Sacrifice, and so, dearest Lord, every day Thou art sacrificed again."

praise,' and no doubt the words retain their ancient meaning:[1] further since Andrewes put out his formal reply to Bellarmine: "do ye Romanists take your transubstantiation out of the Mass, and we shall have no further dispute with you about the Sacrifice,"[2] a succession of English theologians in every century have taught the doctrine with sufficient clearness, and it has had a more prominent position restored to it in the Eucharistic offices (which have sprung from the English) of the Scotch and American Churches. All this is true, but it does not amount to a denial that our Liturgy and formulas suffered in this respect from the influence of unguarded reaction.

We can trace the influence of a similar reaction in the silence of our Church's formularies about the primitive practice of prayers for the blessed departed—a reaction in this case from the excesses of the doctrine of purgatory and indulgences. Once again a similar reaction has robbed us for a time of (to say the least of it) the

---

[1] I think it is only later associations of Protestantism which can lead us to doubt this. The sacrifice of the Mass had been called the 'sacrifice of praise' in Latin, and Eucharist (thanksgiving) in Greek. It was so called because we are not in it 'pleading for admission within the veil,' but claiming, or praising God for, a privilege already won in the acceptance of Christ. Also there is no doubt that the words 'remembrance' in the catechism and 'memory' in the consecration prayer bear naturally their old meaning of a commemoration before God : so Andrewes interprets the word 'memory' (*Respons. ad Bellarm.* p. 251). For the use of the word I should like to refer to the *Theologia Naturalis* of a later schoolman, Raymund of Sabunde (Tit. 289), which affords remarkable analogies to the Anglican consecration prayer as his Tit. 287 (latter part) does to the 'prayer of humble access.'

[2] Andrewes' *Responsio ad Bellarminum* p. 250 f.

immense spiritual convenience of Reservation for the sick, an undoubtedly primitive practice, and of the apostolic practice of Unction of the sick.[1]

These are grave defects—who shall deny it? They are due in part to the temper of compromise, in part, as we say, to the influence of reaction unrestrained by a satisfactory knowledge of ancient doctrine. But if heresy be, as it undoubtedly is, nothing short of the *rejection* of some part of the ancient heritage of truth, the English church is not heretical. She has rejected no truth. Her divines have taught it all. It is being more and more completely taught within her pale to-day. And when we speak of defects in the teaching of the English Church, we must remember for our comfort that the English Church never made a claim to be the whole Church. She never claimed infallibility in her isolated utterances. She always appeals back behind herself to the Scriptures and the ancient Church. A part of a greater whole, she is to us only an authority, so far as, and because, she echoes the voice of what is greater than herself, the universal Church. The defectiveness of the formularies of the 16th and 17th centuries (granting them to be not heretical) are no

[1] The Anglican Confirmation Office is wanting in clear doctrine. But here we propagate (and perhaps exaggerate) an inherited defectiveness of statement which, judged by primitive standards, apparently characterized the mediæval theology on this subject. See the treatise of Canon Mason (Longmans 1891), *The relation of Confirmation to Baptism*. I do not think much apology is needed for our restricted use of the term Sacrament, if Confirmation is regarded as completing Baptism. It is a question of a name. Till the twelfth century the Western Church spoke of *three* sacraments, Baptism, Chrism, and the Eucharist. See my *Dissertations* (Murray) p. 265.

more to us—except in the way of temporary inconvenience—than the defectiveness of the formularies of any other particular moment of the Church's life. The whole Church is our mother. It is the doctrinal heritage of the whole Church that now in the days of completer knowledge, as the mists clear away, is coming out in its indissoluble coherence before the eyes of men, and being taught to the children of the Church.

In this defence of the English Church, I have frankly admitted all the faults of undiscipline, doctrinal compromise and reaction which we think can be fairly laid to our Church's charge. I believe that these are to be set over-against the arrogant claims, the exaggerations of truth, the falsifications of history, the accretions of error, which must be laid to the charge of Rome. Which set of faults is the greater—which Church is more guilty in the eyes of God—it is not for us to determine, it is not our business to attempt to determine.[1] The evils of a Church into which by God's providence we were new-born, granted she *be* a Church, are not an excuse for leaving her, but a spur to action. And I am sure that we Anglicans feel a hearty thankfulness to Almighty God, that He has caused our lot to be cast in a Church, which, however deeply she has sinned, can acknowledge her sins; which, however great her defects even in her authoritative formulas, is not prevented, by any arrogation to herself of what belongs to a greater whole, from confessing them and openly

---

[1] Of course it is not to be forgotten that in the case of undue reaction the blame is divided between those who suffer themselves to react unrestrainedly and those who cause the reaction.

seeking to reform them. Better anything than to be unable to bear the light: better anything than to be unable to face the facts of history and frankly accept them: better any evils than to have to speak deceitfully for God.

Further than this, however much there may be to be regretted and reformed in the teaching and practice of the Anglican Church at the present day, I must in fairness say that there is no even unauthorized practice of the English Church which I had not as soon be responsible for, as for that withdrawal of the chalice from the laity, to which the whole authority of the Church of Rome is committed:—that I have never heard a sermon in an English Church more to be regretted than one it was once my lot to hear in Strasburg Cathedral, in which Christ was preached as the revelation of Divine justice and Mary as the revelation of Divine love: I have not read in Anglican biography anything which I should more desire to disown than Mother Margaret Mary Hallahan's description of the Pope saying Mass:—" When I heard him sing Mass I cannot express what I felt: it was the God of earth prostrate in adoration before the God of heaven"![1] I have not been confronted in an Anglican book of devotion with any prayer more impossible to pray than

> Soul of the Virgin, illuminate me;
> Body of the Virgin, guard me;
> Milk of the Virgin, feed me;
> Passage of the Virgin, strengthen me;
> O Mary, mother of grace, intercede for me;
> For thy servant take me;

[1] *The Life of Mother Margaret Mary Hallahan* (with a preface by Bishop Ullathorne) p. 430.

> Make me always to trust in thee;
> From all evils protect me;
> In the hour of my death assist me;
> And prepare for me a safe way to thee;
> That with all the elect I may glorify thee;
> For ever and ever."[1]

Thus, all things considered, we Anglicans thank God that He has put us elsewhere than in the Roman Church, though we would fain give her an ungrudging recognition of her glories, and are very far from believing that all even of her educated members need be conscious of that temper in her modern theology which to us is so intolerable.

There is only one further remark which it seems desirable to make.

It may seem to some people that the frank recognition of errors and corruptions in every part of the Church impairs our reverence for her as a whole. If we are able to deny this, it is because we believe that the imperfections in the Church do not prevent her fulfilling her true function, and that our reverence for her is not as our reverence for Christ; it is our reverence for the Bride of Christ, not yet purified—for the organ of the Holy Spirit, not yet perfect. The Church exists not yet to exhibit her glory, save to the eye of faith. As for that vision of the Church in her perfection of unity and truth and holiness, the 'city which lieth four-square,' the 'new Jerusalem descending from God out of heaven, prepared as a bride adorned for her husband,' it is the vision of heaven but the hope of

---

[1] *Vade Mecum piorum sacerdotum.* Nova Editio. Campidonæ, 1865. I have translated the prayer.

earth—we shall see it but not now, we shall behold it but not nigh. Meanwhile we have each and all of us all we can want to satisfy our souls with grace and truth, to inspire us for fresh efforts in the cause of God and His kingdom, to draw us out of the world into the communion of the saints, to fit us for the life of heaven. The errors of the Churches have not any way impaired the treasure of the catholic faith. We will borrow words of striking force to express our meaning.

"At sight of this audacity," says the Abbé Gratry at the conclusion of the second of his great letters against the Papal Infallibility—" at the sight of this audacity and this power of falsehood introducing itself into theology, . . . I can understand that all those who do not take in the whole of the questions should be seized with giddiness, and cry out, 'What, then, can we believe now? What becomes of the bases of the faith?'

"I hasten to give a brief and peremptory reply to this objection, which, I think, will satisfy any mind, the most simple as well as the most learned.

"It is, that all these falsehoods and all these frauds tend only to one point, a single one, and in no way to any other. The treasure of the Catholic Faith is here in no way in question. 'We bear this treasure,' says St. Paul, 'in earthen vessels.' Well! all the falsehoods of which I have already spoken, and all those of which I shall speak, affect the vessel and not the treasure. Our treasure is Jesus Christ, His Gospel, His real Presence, the Eucharist, Penance, and the Remission of sin; the dogma of the Communion of the Saints, the visible existence of the Holy Church, our Mother; the fact of eternal life, the life divine and supernatural, conferred upon souls when this life is over. This treasure is immaculate, entire, certain, incontestable beyond the reach of frauds and doubts. Fear nothing, Christian souls! Feed upon the divine life, the sources of which are known to you. In every village of every Christian country, the priest of Jesus Christ holds the keys of the Church, into which you may enter to recline as the Apostle St. John did, upon the bosom of the Saviour Jesus, and you can ask of Him His soul, His heart, His blood, His mind, His divinity; this is our treasure. It will not be taken from us."

The Abbé Gratry is right. In spite of falsehoods, in spite of compromise, the catholic Church is still in every place the treasure-house of all the grace and truth which is the legacy of Jesus Christ to His redeemed.

CHAPTER XI

THREE RECENT PAPAL UTTERANCES

THREE recent Papal utterances, all of them considerably later in date than the first issue of this little book (1888), have illustrated so forcibly features in the character and method of the Roman Church to which attention was called in these pages, that it seems to be desirable to take notice of them in a concluding chapter.

I.

The Encyclical (of 1893) on "the Study of Sacred Scripture."

1. The motive of the Encyclical is "to give an impulse to the noble science of Holy Scripture and to impart to Scripture study a direction suitable to the needs of the present day." Thus the bulk of the Encyclical is an exhortation to the study of Holy Scripture by ecclesiastical persons. This is recommended, by arguments such as can easily be imagined, from the authority of our Lord Himself, of St. Peter and the other Apostles, of the Fathers, and of the later Church, of which it is said :—

"She has prescribed that a considerable portion of the sacred books shall be read and piously reflected upon by all her ministers in the daily office of the sacred psalmody. She has ordered that in cathedral churches, in monasteries, and in other convents in which study can conveniently be pursued, they shall be expounded and interpreted by capable men; and she has strictly commanded that her children shall be fed with the saving words of the Gospel at least on Sundays and solemn feasts. Moreover, it is owing to the wisdom and exertions of the Church that there has always been continued from century to century that cultivation of Holy Scripture which has been so remarkable and borne such ample fruit."

But none the less there is need of further encouragement in this study at the present moment in view of the perils which beset it.

There follows a description of the rationalism which by a natural evolution has taken the place of the older assertion of the right of private judgment as the chief antagonist of the Catholic Church.

The rationalistic critics are described in language applicable only to those who deny altogether the existence and action of supernatural influence, but allusion is made also to would-be theologians and Christians who "attempt to disguise by such honourable names their rashness and their pride"; and there has been a previous allusion to men (apparently within the Church) who "attempt innovations in a deceitful and imprudent spirit."

It is noticed how the attacks of rationalism are not confined to the academic region, but that "the efforts and arts of the enemy are chiefly directed against the more ignorant masses of the people" by every method of propaganda.

Later on an account is given of the principle of

current criticism, with which (apart from the extraordinary exaggeration of the last sentence) many of us would sympathize in part:—

"There has arisen, to the great detriment of religion, an inept method, dignified by the name of 'higher criticism,' which pretends to judge of the origin, integrity, and authority of each book from internal indications alone. It is clear, on the other hand, that in historical questions, such as the origin or the handing down of writings, the witness of history is of primary importance, and that historical investigation should be made with the utmost care; and that in this matter internal evidence is seldom of great value, except as confirmation."

Then Orientalists are not very tenderly dealt with:—

"It is a lamentable fact that there are many who, with great labour, carry out and publish investigations on the monuments of antiquity, the manners and institutions of nations, and other illustrative subjects, and whose chief purpose in all this is too often to find mistakes in the sacred writings, and so to shake and weaken their authority."

Such are the conditions which postulate a fresh access of ecclesiastical zeal in the "scientific" study and interpretation of Holy Scripture. The Vulgate version is to be the main standard of study and reference, but recourse to the original languages is declared to be "useful and advantageous" in cases where the meaning is ambiguous or less clear. The literal sense is to be held to where possible, but legitimate allegorical interpretation is also to be employed as having an authority even apostolic.

In all this there is nothing much to surprise us. It is what we should expect in a Papal Encyclical. It would be practically valuable if it produced an increased study of Holy Scripture on the part of ecclesiastics: What is remarkable is the doctrine consistently enunciated as to the character of Biblical inspiration. The Vatican Council, following Trent, expressly defined that the books of the Old and New Testaments "have God for their *auctor*." But Newman[1] and others had interpreted "auctor" as meaning no more than "primary cause." Now, however, the Pope declares God their author in such simple and positive sense that any error in the sacred text would involve "that God Himself was deceived":—

"It is true, no doubt, that copyists have made mistakes in the text of the Bible ; this question, when it arises, should be carefully considered on its merits, and the fact not too easily admitted, but only in those passages where the proof is clear. It may also happen that the sense of a passage remains ambiguous, and in this case good hermeneutical methods will greatly assist in clearing up the obscurity. But it is absolutely wrong and forbidden, either to narrow inspiration to certain parts only of Holy Scripture, or to admit that the sacred writer has erred. For the system of those who, in order to rid themselves of these difficulties, do not hesitate to concede that divine inspiration regards the things of faith and morals, and nothing beyond, because (as they wrongly think), in a question of the truth or falsehood of a passage, we should consider not so much what God has said as the reason and purpose which He had in mind in saying it—this system cannot be tolerated. For all the books which the Church receives as sacred and canonical are written wholly and entirely, with all their parts, at the dictation of the Holy Ghost ; and so far is it from being possible that any error can co-exist with inspiration, that inspiration not only is essentially incompatible with error, but excludes and

[1] *Nineteenth Century*, February 1884, p. 188.

rejects it as absolutely and necessarily as it is impossible that God Himself, the supreme Truth, can utter that which is not true. This is the ancient and unchanging faith of the Church, solemnly defined in the Councils of Florence and Trent, and finally confirmed and more expressly formulated by the Council of the Vatican. These are the words of the last :—

"The Books of the Old and New Testament, whole and entire, with all their parts, as enumerated in the decree of the same Council (Trent) and in the ancient Latin Vulgate, are to be received as sacred and canonical. And the Church holds them as sacred and canonical, not because, having been composed by human industry, they were afterwards approved by her authority; nor only because they contain revelation without error; but because, having been written under the inspiration of the Holy Ghost, they have God for their author.

Hence, because the Holy Ghost employed men as His instruments, we cannot, therefore, say that it was these inspired instruments who, perchance, have fallen into error, and not the primary Author. For, by supernatural power, He so moved and impelled them to write—He was so present to them—that the things which he ordered, and those only, they first rightly understood, then willed faithfully to write down, and finally expressed in apt words and with infallible truth. Otherwise, it could not be said that He was the Author of the entire Scripture. Such has always been the persuasion of the Fathers. 'Therefore,' says St. Augustine, 'since they wrote the things which He showed and uttered to them, it cannot be pretended that He is not the writer; for His members executed what their Head dictated.' And St. Gregory the Great thus pronounces :—

"Most superfluous it is to inquire who wrote these things—we loyally believe the Holy Ghost to be the Author of the book. He wrote it Who dictated it for writing; He wrote it Who inspired its execution.

"It follows that those who maintain that an error is possible in any genuine passage of the sacred writings either pervert the Catholic notion of inspiration, or make God the author of such error. And so emphatically were all the Fathers and Doctors agreed that the Divine writings, as left by the hagiographers, are free from all error, that they laboured earnestly, with no less skill than reverence, to reconcile with each other those numerous passages which seem at variance—the very passages which in great measure have been taken up by the 'higher criticism'; for they were unanimous in laying it down, that those writings, in their entirety and in all their parts, were equally from the *afflatus* of Almighty God, and that God, speaking by the sacred writers, could not set down anything but what was true. The words of St. Augustine to St. Jerome may sum up what they taught :—

"On my own part I confess to your charity that it is only to those books of Scripture which are now called canonical that I have learned to pay such honour and reverence as to believe most firmly that none of their writers has fallen into any error. And if in these books I meet anything which seems contrary to truth, I shall not hesitate to conclude either that the text is faulty, or that the translator has not expressed the meaning of the passage, or that I myself do not understand it."

This passage is most remarkable. It is nothing whatever but an assertion by the Pope of "verbal inspiration" as the indubitable doctrine of the Church. Naturally, therefore, he condemns unhesitatingly any limitation of inspiration, in the sense in which it involves infallibility, to the things of faith and morals, and (by implication) the accompanying recognition of grades of inspiration. Yet this is, I believe, a new departure and of great importance. Newman had remarked that[1] :—

"While the Councils (of Trent and the Vatican) lay down so emphatically the inspiration of Scripture in respect to 'faith and morals,' it is remarkable that they do not say a word directly as to its inspiration in matters of fact." "Four times does the Tridentine Council insist upon 'faith and morality' as the scope of inspired teaching." "In like manner the Vatican Council pronounces that supernatural revelation consists '*in rebus Divinis.*'"

[1] *l.c.*, p. 189.

Newman emphasizes this, though he rejects the large conclusion that "the record of facts does not come under the guarantee of inspiration." When we pass from Councils to Popes, here again it would appear that the see of Rome[1] had maintained silence on the questions raised within the Roman communion as to the limits of inspiration—a silence which might be described as studious. Thus in Canon di Bartolo's useful work, *Critères Theologiques*,[2] it is laid down as the positive proposition that—

"Inspiration is a supernatural succour which flows in upon the intelligence and will of the sacred writer, and causes him to write the true doctrine in matter of faith and morality, the true facts which are inseparably connected with them, and everything else with a right intention and a Divine mission of a quite special character for the salvation of the human race."

Thus the doctrine of *grades* of inspiration, the idea of an inspiration which does not guarantee infallibility, and the limitation of the highest sort of infallibility to things of faith and morals and what is inseparably allied with them—all this is expressly declared by the moderate theologian we are quoting an open and allowed doctrine. An apparently increasing body of Roman writers have been acting on the assumption that it was open doctrine. But now it is utterly condemned by the authority of the Pope. The Encyclical asserts as beyond all question that, when once the right text is ascertained and the sense plain, all possibility of error of any kind is excluded, because the omniscient and

[1] See Manning's *Temporal Mission of the Holy Ghost*, p. 138.
[2] French translation from the Italian, pp. 244-258.

infallible God is the real author of the text; with the result that it is "nothing to the point that the Holy Spirit should have employed human instruments, as if anything erroneous could have escaped not from the primary author, but from the inspired writers," for the Holy Spirit actually dictated all the words.

In the Encyclical then, we witness, as it appears, an entire victory of the school of extreme theologians (such as would be represented by Cornely, the leading author of the recent Jesuit *Scripturae sacrae cursus*) who have been trying of recent years to tie the Roman Church to the scholastic rigorism as to the meaning of inspiration.

2. What is the authority which from a Roman Catholic point of view this Encyclical Letter possesses? Is it an utterance of the Pope *ex cathedrâ*, and, therefore, infallible? The Pope is infallible when, "speaking as head of the Church, and in the plenitude of his supreme authority, he defines a doctrine of faith and morals which must be accepted by all Bishops and all the faithful."[1] Provided that the intention of defining authoritatively is clear, a bull, an encyclical, an apostolic letter, a brief, a local council, may be the vehicle of the infallible utterance. Is the Pope in this encyclical expressing a clear intention to define the meaning of the doctrine of inspiration for all Bishops and for all the faithful? One would suppose so from the tone of the letter. But perhaps it would be said that the definition is only assumed by the way as a basis for practical exhortation. No doubt some reason may be

[1] Di Bartolo, p. 93.

found—has, in fact, been found—to declare the Encyclical not infallible, in the same way that the *Decretum* of Eugenius to the Armenians about holy order or the Bull *Unam Sanctam*, so far as it affects the temporal power of sovereigns, has been declared not infallible, having been found in fact erroneous or impracticable. The definition of what are the conditions of *ex cathedrâ* utterances is most conveniently vague in any statement of them, whether Franzelin's or Di Bartolo's. I confine myself, then, to the recognition of the fact that the Pope, being believed to be what he is believed to be in the Roman Church, has proclaimed with absolute decision and complete authoritativeness of tone, as the doctrine of the Church, the doctrine of the exact verbal inspiration of Holy Scripture.

3. This Papal utterance appears to be, from the point of view of one who desires to see a reconciliation of Christian theology with scientific criticism, most disastrous. Let any one read the wise, guarded words of the French theologian M. Loisy, on *la Question Biblique* in what was (alas!) the last number of his periodical *L'Enseignement Biblique*, and estimate what a calamity it is that this utterance of authority should have put an end to the periodical with the ending of the year 1893.[1] The fact is symbolical. It is designed to suppress the school of free and real criticism which seemed to be forming itself in the Roman Church, and

[1] The following *Avis* is prefixed to the last issue :—'*L'Enseignement Biblique* ne paraîtra pas en 1894. Fidèlement soumis aux dernières instructions du souverain Pontif Léon XIII., le directeur de la revue éprouve le besoin de se récueiller quelque temps dans un travail silencieux.'

taking such firm root. Nothing is to be allowed—as far as the Pope can secure it—but such apologetics as can be based on the assumption that there are no discrepancies, even minute, between Kings and Chronicles, or one part of the Bible and another (when once the true text is ascertained) that alike the narrative of Genesis i.-xi., and that of Daniel, nay, those of Tobit and Judith, are in the strict sense historical, and that the Pentateuchal Legislation, as put into the mouth of Moses, is all strictly Mosaic. Nothing else is to be allowed—till truth revenges itself as it revenged itself on the same Church when she dealt in similar fashion with the science of Galileo.[1]

4. This is all sad and disheartening enough from the wider point of view. The decision, however, may help to make it apparent that the Anglican Church has, as was suggested above,[2] apart from its ordinary mission to the English-speaking races, a mission of a more special sort, as that part of the Church where faith and free science must win their reconciliation. We should suppose that this Encyclical would have a dissuasive power on persons disposed to put their trust in Rome, if they have any interest in the relation of faith to contemporary knowledge. No document could present more emphatically the spectacle of a great ruler failing to deal with a situation—failing indeed, marvellously,

---

[1] It should be noticed that the tone of the Encyclical is much more guarded when it proceeds to speak of the relation of Holy Scripture to physical science: see the authorized translation (Burns and Oates), p. 21 ff.

[2] Pp. 14-15.

utterly—than this Encyclical of the Pope to the Bishops of the Roman Catholic communion. It is written as by a being inhabiting a planet different from that which is the scene of modern knowledge. What must be said of a Church which, while making the highest profession of guidance through a chief pastor, has nothing better than this to offer on one of the most difficult subjects that strain the religious thought of the present? There is not a word said, such as one would expect from any Catholic source, of the way in which the Catholic creed focuses the rays of Holy Scripture on a single Person, and exhibits it all, not as a flat surface of uniform level, but as a district of very varying levels and gradients converging upon a city and a sanctuary. The way of regarding the Bible which some describe as purely Protestant appears here to be (what, in fact, students have always known it to be) a product of mediæval scholasticism. All that Renan meant when he said that a student of Holy Scripture would find that "the little finger of the [Roman] Catholic Church is thicker than the loins of Protestantism" is here shown true enough. It cannot, in fact, be conceived how a document more out of date, more crude, more unsympathetic, more unpastoral than the present Encyclical could have been issued. And if the Romans succeed in minimizing its importance, and reassert their liberty to pursue the critical study of Holy Scripture, they only minimize the importance of their chief pastor. All he could do to give authoritative guidance he has done. And the guidance is—what here appears.

It remains, then, for us to try and do better. And we can depend upon it that it is in proportion as we can positively exhibit a catholic life which is open to modern knowledge, which can assimilate its fruits with faith and devotion unimpaired, that we can best minister in the final result to the reunion of Christendom. We must become all that we have it in us to be; and moral needs, both personal and social, as well as the intellectual gains and difficulties of the present, alike give us our opportunity.

II.

The Encyclical on Unity, "Satis Cognitum" (1896).

This Encyclical, though intrinsically less important than the one just discussed, has excited much more attention, owing to the attention which Leo XIII. had been bestowing upon the "recovery of England."

The principle of ecclesiastical unity in the visible Church is stated in the opening portions of this Encyclical in a manner thoroughly consonant to the ancient idea of the apostolic succession, in accordance with which all the bishops are equally successors of the Apostles. From the earlier portion the Cyprianic or Anglican doctrine of the authority of the Episcopal College would naturally follow. The familiar papal conclusion is, however, drawn from the consideration that every society must have a supreme authority which must reside in one person. Nothing is more remarkable than the assumption which henceforth pervades the Encyclical that "only a despotic monarch can secure to any society unity and strength." This premiss once granted, it follows easily enough that Christ should have appointed Peter Head of the Church, and given him succession in the bishops of Rome.

The rest of the Encyclical expresses the papal claim in its most familiar form. The arguments have been already dealt with in earlier chapters.[1] It is only necessary here to notice some characteristic features of the document.

1. *Its arbitrary assumptions* :—

"The nature of this supreme authority, which all Christians are bound to obey, can be ascertained only by finding out what was the evident and positive Will of Christ. Certainly Christ is a King for ever, and, though invisible, He continues unto the end of time to govern and guard His Church from heaven. But since He willed that His Kingdom should be visible, He was obliged, when He ascended into heaven, to designate a Vicegerent on earth."

How can it be known that Christ must have acted in this particular way? Is not this just the point where careful examination of the earliest Christian documents is needed, to see what was the evident will of Christ? Is not the suggestion of the Pope as to how Christ must have acted, constituting the Church on earth a body complete in itself, with a visible head, in remarkable contrast to the view of St. Augustine, given at length above[2]—a view simply representative of the ancient idea of local Churches, associated in fellowship on earth, but finding their necessary centre of unity, in

[1] See further *The Encyclical Satis Cognitum*, published for the Ch. Hist. Soc. by S.P.C.K.
[2] Page 34.

common with the Church in paradise, at no lower point than in the glorified Christ?

2. *Its wholly unhistorical assertions :—*

"The consent of antiquity ever acknowledged without the slightest doubt or hesitation the bishops of Rome, and revered them as the legitimate successors of St. Peter."

What a marvellous assertion, in view of the fact that (as shown at length above) the papal claim of the succession to Petrine privileges is a purely Western growth. It does not appear[1] that a single Greek Father of the first six centuries recognizes the connection, which is the corner-stone of the Roman claim, between Christ's promise to St. Peter and the position of the Pope. "In the writings of the Greek doctors," says "Janus," "Eusebius, St. Athanasius, St. Basil the Great, the two Gregories, and St. Epiphanius, there is no one word of any [unique] prerogative of the Roman bishop. The most copious of the Greek Fathers, St. Chrysostom, is wholly silent on the subject." What, then, is the meaning of talking of the "consent of antiquity," or of describing the decrees of the Vatican Council as "the venerable and constant belief of every age"? (We may notice in passing that the Encyclical gives no recognition at all to the principle of "development of doctrine.") What, again, is the meaning of saying that "it has ever been unquestionably the office of the Roman pontiffs to ratify or to reject the decrees of Councils," when, as late as the fifteenth century Council of Constance, the subordination of Popes to Councils[2] was unmistakably asserted as the doctrine of the Church?

[1] See p. 91.   [2] See p. 122.

THREE RECENT PAPAL UTTERANCES. 199

3. *Its unjustifiable quotations:*—Of these I will content myself with giving three instances—(*a*) The Pope quotes St. Pacian as saying, "To Peter the Lord spake; to *one* therefore, that He might establish unity upon one." But he omits to mention that he continues, "And soon he was to give the same injunction to the general body." (*b*) He cites, in confirmation of the papal view of Peter as the rock, some quite ambiguous words of Origen, to the effect that no more against the rock, than against the Church, can the gates of hell prevail, although the passage cited above[1] immediately precedes, which proves conclusively that Origen had no idea that Peter had any privilege which all the other Apostles did not share. (*c*) He cites St. Cyprian as saying "of the Roman Church that 'It is the root and mother of the Catholic Church, the Chair of Peter, and the principal Church whence sacerdotal unity had its origin.'" This is a combination of two different passages, of which the first, "the root and mother of the Catholic Church," has no reference to the Roman Church, and the second, from a letter strongly rebuking the Pope, refers to Rome as the source of the apostolical succession in Africa.[2]

Now I may fairly ask whether the accusations of inveracity and disingenuousness which have been made in the course of this book against the Roman method of argument, are not again justified?

III.

The Bull "Apostolicae Curae."

Within the last few months the Pope has issued the

[1] See p. 86.   [2] See p. 118.

above bull, condemning our orders as "absolutely null and utterly void."

The bulk of this document is occupied with deciding that the question was not an open one for Roman Catholics, the Roman Church having already determined it. Disputable as this position may be, we are not concerned with it,[1] but, fortunately for us, the Pope is not contented with reasserting a negative attitude, but gives his reasons. As regards these reasons given, then, we notice that there is a marked abandonment of old grounds—not the "Nag's Head" fable only, but the denial also that Barlow was a bishop, and the position of Eugenius as to the form and matter of holy order.[2] All these objections are—the first two tacitly, the last explicitly—abandoned. But

(1) Anglican orders are repudiated,[3] because there was not in the Edwardine service for ordaining priests[4] explicit mention, in the words of ordination, of the office of priesthood to which ordination was being conferred, and more precisely, of "the power of consecrating and offering the true body and blood of the Lord," *i.e.* in the Eucharistic sacrifice.

But it is manifest, from the existing services of ordination, that the specification of this function of the priesthood is equally absent, not only from the

---

[1] See above, p. 141. [2] See above, pp. 142-9.
[3] This matter is here very briefly dealt with, because *The Bull Apostolicae Curae and the Edwardine Ordinal* (Puller) and *A Treatise on the Bull Apostolicae Curae* (Ch. Hist. Soc., S.P.C.K.) have said everything which needs to be said upon the subject, in as brief compass and as well as possible.
[4] See above, p. 150 and note 1.

Coptic rite, but also from the ancient Roman rite for ordination to the priesthood in the third century, and later down to the ninth century. If the absence of this specification invalidates ordinations, they were indeed invalidated long before the English Church came into existence. Here, in fact, we touch upon a matter of importance. Confessedly the English Church desired to return to the richer and fuller conception of the function of the priest which had prevailed in primitive times, before the function of offering sacrifice had assumed the undue prominence given to it in the Middle Ages. "Be thou a faithful dispenser of the Word of God and of His holy Sacraments" includes, no doubt, the commission to celebrate the Eucharistic sacrifice, but it puts it in context with the whole work of the ministry, according to primitive models and scriptural ideas. Of such a return to antiquity we have no reason to be ashamed, and the Edwardine ordinal makes it abundantly manifest, that the office which is being conferred is nothing else than the office of the priesthood. The Pope must indeed have been dreaming when he said that "in the whole ordinal there is no clear mention of . . . the priesthood"[1]

(2) Passing by a similar objection to the ordination of a bishop, which falls on the same grounds, we find the Pope asserting that the intention of the Anglican Church was inadequate, owing to the defective ideas of the priesthood which her offices express. But here nothing new is alleged. The only requisite intention is the intention to continue the orders which had been

[1] See the *Treatise on the Bull*, pp. 20-28.

all along in the Church, the general intention of continuing to do what the Church in general had done;[1] and so understood the Church of England made her intention perfectly clear. The views of particular men cannot be brought into question, and no requirement can be legitimately made that the Church of England should have been in express agreement with the doctrine current in the Church of Rome at one particular epoch. All this has been argued above.

The real significance of this Bull lies in the fact that a school of liberal Roman Catholic theologians had been within the last few years candidly examining the question of Anglican orders and one after another expressing their belief more or less decisively in their validity; and the Bull is only one more example of the refusal of Rome to sanction free and impartial inquiry into historical facts. The tenor of the Encyclical about Holy Scripture and, of the Bull just considered, is in fact identical. They go together to confirm that view of the Roman spirit which our whole inquiry has forced us to take. But this conclusion—that Rome is inadequate to represent the original purpose and meaning of the Christian Church in tolerable completeness,—should be to us Anglicans a motive to nothing else than a humble, prayerful, and continual effort to realize better in our own branch of the Church the high vocation to which we are called.

[1] See above, p. 156.

APPENDED NOTE I.

THE BEARING OF THE THEORY OF DEVELOPMENT ON CHRISTIAN DOCTRINE.[1]

No doubt the idea of evolution is a dominant idea in our time. In order to render anything intelligible to ourselves we need to regard it as part of a connected process, either as a result, or as a stage which "looks before and after," and which is to be viewed in the light of that out of which it has grown, and that into which it is passing. In other words, we expect with reference to all subjects an answer, not to the simple question, "What is it?" but rather to the threefold question, "Whence comes it," and " whither goes it," and "by what law?" The effect of this idea of evolution on theology is necessarily important. I may illustrate it by three examples.

(1) It changes our natural way of thinking about God's revelation of Himself. It makes it harder for us to think of revealed truth as a detached and definite body of propositions of equal value given within a certain area of time and space, and it inclines us to think of God as revealing Himself by a gradual process which embraces in a certain sense the whole world, and the whole of human history, which has its initial and imperfect stages, but which has also among the chosen people its region of special intensity, and in Jesus Christ and Pentecost its point of culmination. But in this respect it is perhaps truer to say that modern modes of thought tend to make us, not adopt a new way of thinking about revelation, but recur to an older one.

(2) It modifies our way of thinking about eschatology or

[1] An Address delivered at the Church Congress, Shrewsbury, October 1896.

"the doctrine of the last things." There are two ways of thinking about the results of human lives. You may think of men as receiving beyond the grave rewards or punishments, given from outside by the Divine Judge; or you may think of each human life as perpetually occupied in fashioning its own character, and thus also, according to inevitable law, its own ultimate destiny. These two ways of thinking are not inconsistent. The inevitable outcome may be also the divinely allotted reward or penalty, but in any case the idea of evolution forces us first of all to the latter of the two modes of thinking about the issues of human lives. Whatever is to be our state hereafter, we are quite sure it will only be the natural outgrowth of what we are or are making ourselves here and now.

(3) The idea of evolution has resulted in that way of studying Christian doctrine which is specially exemplified in German *Histories of Dogma*. Dr. Hatch used to complain that theologians would quote all ancient fathers as if they were isolated atoms on a uniform level, whether it were Justin Martyr, or Leo the Great, Gregory of Nyssa, or Gregory of Rome. But this way of quoting the fathers must vanish even from regions where it still flourishes. To each writer must be assigned his "value," by having always in mind the place he occupies in the development of theology in some particular part of the world.

Evolution, then, has taken hold of theology. It has modified our way of thinking about it. It will not be dislodged. But before it became thus broadly an established principle of theological knowledge, it had received a certain controversial application; for in the book which first familiarized the English public with the application of development to theology, a book which we must remember preceded by fifteen years the publication of Darwin's *Origin of Species*—I mean, of course, Newman's *Essay on the Development of Christian Doctrine*—the idea of evolution (or development) in theology was used to justify the position of the Church of Rome. Quiet thought on the subject seems to me continually to deepen our perception of the varied application of the idea of evolution to theology—sometimes in ways which Newman would have refused to recognize—while at the same time it weakens the force of the particular application of it which Newman suggested. We may find an analogy for this conclusion in the history of the idea of evolution as applied to nature as a whole. There, too, we may distinguish between the general idea and one particular controversial application of it. The general idea has deepened and strengthened its hold on our minds in every region of inquiry; but the particular controversial application of it, viz. as a sufficient and final answer to the theist's time-honoured "argument from design," has from various causes been weakened rather than strengthened in lapse of time. So it has been in theology; and it is to this particular application of the subject that I proceed to devote myself.

Newman's argument may be in general terms summarized thus:—Christianity came into the world as an idea or a germ. It was planted there to grow. It has grown, and in lapse of time has become the Roman Catholic Church, which is a result of a continuous organic growth over a wide area and on a great scale. And it is the only great growth. The Eastern Church represents a backwater as compared to a current, or a formula as compared to a living principle; Protestantism represents an individualist reaction rather than a growth; and Anglicanism a somewhat hopeless appeal to antiquity in place of a living grasp on the present. I have stated this argument in extreme form, only because for my present purposes I am going to grant all it claims, as if it were a fair statement of the case. Granted, then, for the purposes of argument that the facts are so, may we conclude that because the Roman Catholic Church is the main actual development of Christianity, therefore it is justified in claiming to be the authenticated representative of primitive Christianity? Is what an idea historically becomes necessarily the true interpretation of it? The answer to this question, which may be derived from the history of religions, is a most emphatic No. Nothing is more conspicuous there than the tendency to deterioration, or the tendency on the part of a religion to change character by gradual self-accommodation to circumstances instead of moulding circumstances in accordance with its original idea. This fact is apparent in the history of Buddhism. No mistake could be so vital as to take the main existing developments of Buddhism as really interpreting the spirit of Sakya Muni. But it may be said the divine presence in Christianity guarantees us against perversion or distortion of the original type. We must look to facts: and first to the history of the Old Covenant. Devotion to the Mosaic law, as divinely given, reached its climax at the return from the Captivity. It was kindled into a splendid enthusiasm through the heroism of the Maccabean period. Then it developed into the Judaism of our Lord's time. That was beyond question its main and substantial growth. Thus when John the Baptist appeared, he appeared as a protestant against the actual development which the inspired religion had received; as one "throwing back" to an earlier prophetic type. Nay, more, when the Christ, the divinely intended result of the Old Covenant, appeared, the representatives of the actual development repudiated and crucified Him; and Christ had already interpreted this fact in His own attitude towards tradition. Tradition, He said, had misled the scribes and Pharisees, because they had not continually tested it by the "Word of God." "Thus have ye made the commandment of God of none effect by your tradition." I draw from this a certain conclusion, namely, that a religion, because divinely inspired, is not therefore preserved from widespread deterioration; is not therefore prevented from receiving a development which, while it must appear as the chief historical development of the original, is in fact its parody. I apply this conclusion to Christianity. Christ indeed did promise that His presence and His Spirit, the Spirit both of truth and grace, should never fail in the Church, and that promise has been verified. The truth essential to make Christian saints has always been shining in the world through the witness of the Christian Church, and the power to correspond with the divine requirements has always been communicated through the means of grace to the sons of faith. There has, therefore, been no failure of Christ's promise. On the other hand, it is only by a misapplication of Christ's promises, precisely similar to that on which the scribes and Pharisees of Judaism based their false and disastrous claim ("We have Abraham to our father"), that the leaders of the Christian Church have lulled themselves into a perilous security against the possibility that the Church, short of substantial failure, may go far astray. There is no guarantee that the Church may not, if she neglects the means provided to keep her right, get upon a false line of development, and that almost universally. Thus, without stopping to dispute all that Newman says about the Roman Church in its relation to primitive Christianity, we may still affirm that the protest of the Reformation may have been as necessary to recall Christianity to its ideal as the protest of John the Baptist was to recall the Judaism of Israel to its right allegiance, and to interpret our Lord's strong depreciation of a mere, or unchecked, ecclesiastical tradition.

And what are the facts about the Roman Church? When you come to look at them it appears self-evident that the Roman development is a development with two characteristics. First, it is partial or one-sided, a development which has left out elements in the original type—the very splendour of its success in dealing with a particular situation or set of situations tended to make it this. Secondly, it is a development which is the result of an over-reckless self-accommodation to the unregenerate natural instincts in religion. I confine myself to one significant illustration of the latter proposition—I mean the development of the cultus of the saints in its mediæval and modern form. It is written on the face of Church history that this has resulted from Christianity accepting, not without preliminary protest, but finally even with enthusiasm, what is simply an almost universal phenomenon of untaught natural religion all over the world. If you travel in many a Buddhist, or Mohammedan, or Christian country, you see the same facts; the same devotion gathering round the tombs of departed saints, who are regarded as intercessors or mediators, and as patrons of particular places or trades or classes, and are approached with divine or semi-divine homage. The tendency, the exhibited devotion, the results of the devotion, are startlingly identical as one observes them in all parts of the world. Now this saint worship was quite alien to the original spirit of Mohammedanism. It was much more alien to the original spirit of Buddhism; but in both cases the dominant, popular instinct has overmastered the original idea, and the alien or repugnant element has taken its place, perhaps its place of supremacy, in the religion which still retains the ancient name of Mohammed or Buddha. Facts irresistibly point to the conclusion that exactly the same thing has occurred in Christianity. The half-converted masses passed into the Church with this dominant instinct of hero worship still in them—with the dominant demand for mediators and objects of worship less high and holy than God. The demand had met with a strong opposition in the maxims and principles of the Christian theology which belongs to the period when struggle and persecution kept Christianity at a high level; but when Christianity became popular, the incoming flood was too large and too rapid to be resisted or properly educated. It had its way, and a saint worship, which belongs essentially to natural and not to revealed religion, and which exhibits all its old phenomena, has taken its place in Christianity. To say that it belongs to natural religion is to say something *for* it. Moreover, there is in revealed religion a principle of the communion of saints which is akin to it. Therefore I am not now saying that there is no legitimate human and Christian cultus of the saints. God forbid. And I am very far from denying that we in the Church of England have far too little of it. All that I am saying is that the actual development of that cultus as it appeared in the mediæval Church is a development of primitive Christianity, but a development in exactly the same sense in which exactly the same product is a development of Mohammedanism or Buddhism.

My first contention, then, is this: there exists in all

religions a tendency to develop by way of deterioration, by way of a one-sided distortion, and by way of a too easy assimilation of elements in the natural instinct of religion which are really uncongenial—at least without deep transformation—to their original idea. My second contention is that these tendencies are indisputably manifest in the actual development of Romanism out of primitive Christianity. My third contention is that the fact that Christianity is in a special sense a revealed or inspired religion, does not secure it against liability to fall into these tendencies, if it is guilty of neglect in using the means which would prevent such a disaster. My proof of this contention lies in pointing to the actual development of the religion of the Old Covenant, and to the significant warning of our Lord that ecclesiastical developments need checking by the Word of God. We are left, then, in this position. We might grant, as fully as Newman, even in his most extreme moments, seems to require it, that existing Romanism is the only real living development of Primitive Christianity on a large scale. And still we should have to reiterate that it does not therefore follow that a position of protest against it is not the position which makes us inheritors of John the Baptist and of our Lord Himself. Of course, in merely animal or vegetable nature, we may say that the existing development is the only, and therefore the divinely-intended, development; but where, as in human history, the fact of sin comes in, we can say nothing of the kind. The existing development of no human society, not even of the Church, necessarily represents the divine intention. What the divine intention for human society in general may be we are left to ascertain, as best we can, by consulting our judgments and our moral ideals. But in regard to the Church we are provided with more definite guidance. The Church is a continuous society with its necessary "tradition," but it has, or ought to have, ever before its eyes a definite and fixed—because written—ideal to which it is to be continually recurring, the evangelical and apostolic type which is, or ought to be, the test of every doctrine, of every institution, of every moral ideal, claiming the allegiance of Christians; and to abandon which, for any reason whatever, is nothing else than faithlessness to the divine word.

Briefly I would conclude by indicating the true idea of Christian development. In the Word made Flesh, in the Church in which God and man are at one, is the climax of all possible religious development. No disclosure of God to man, no union of man with God, can be closer than is here attained. Thus the revelation of Godhead, the revelation of manhood, the deposit of truth and the deposit of grace which are original in Christianity, and find their witness enshrined in the original institutions and tradition of the Church and in the writings of the Apostles—this is final and Catholic. But it takes a special development according to the genius of each race and of each age—for example, in Alexandrian, in Russian, in Celtic, early Irish and Scotch, Christianity, and, greatest of all, in Roman Catholicism. The vital point is that no one of these developments, each necessarily partial, should be allowed so to stereotype itself as to limit the power of recurrence to the original truths and institutions in order to a fresh development for a new race or the needs of a new age. This is the meaning of the "appeal to Scripture."

The doctrines of the Nicene creed, the institutions of the apostolic ministry and the sacraments—these can manifestly make good their appeal to the New Testament. Christianity is a life based both on revealed truths and divinely inaugurated and inspired institutions. The dogmas and institutions that can really be called Catholic are the real interpreters of Scripture. They are no obstacle to the freest appeal to any really original feature in Christianity. These are the elements out of which development is continually to take place afresh in view of changing needs and requirements. And in the fact that, with all our weaknesses and all our failures, we in the Church of England have retained the essential Catholic elements, and, hampered though we are in hand and foot, by the results of our past sins and our miserable subservience to statecraft and to wealth, are yet unfettered by any uncatholic dogma, and are pledged by our whole tradition to the appeal to Scripture—in this fact, I say, there lies the rational ground of a profound belief in the vocation of Anglicanism. The Catholic starting-point is under our feet; the rich experience of the past is stored up to enlighten, but not to enslave us; its old examples of faith and zeal and love have lost none of their inspirations; the needs of the age are clamorous. Can we then "discern the time" we live in, and rise to our vocation?

II

THE CONCEPTION OF CHURCH UNITY IN ST. HILARY.

Cf. p. 32.

THE conception of Church unity explained above in Chapter II. is admirably illustrated by St. Hilary of Poitiers in his argument with the Arians, *de Trin.* viii. 5-8. The Arians interpreted Christ's declaration "I and My Father are one" as referring only to a unity of will or consent, not to a unity of nature, and they justified their interpretation by an appeal to expressions used about the Church such as "of one heart and of one soul"; for the unity of the Church, they said, is also a unity which consists in agreement of wills. But this argument Hilary repudiates, and turns their appeal against themselves. The unity of the Church, he insists, is a unity of nature which exists because all its members are common sharers in the new life of Christ. "They are one through regeneration into the same nature." "The Apostle teaches that the unity of the faithful comes from the nature of the sacraments, when he writes to the Galatians, 'As many of you as were baptized into Christ, have put on Christ. There is neither Jew nor Greek, neither bond nor free, neither male nor female, for ye are all one in Christ Jesus.' This unity, in spite of all differences of race, condition, sex, does it arise from assent of will? Is it not rather sacramental, because they have all received one baptism and been clothed with one Christ? What function then has harmony of mind to fulfil in a case where unity among men is already secured by the fact that they are clothed with the one Christ, through the nature of the one baptism?"

III

ST. BASIL AND ST. HILARY ON DOCTRINAL CONFUSION IN THE CHURCH. *Cf.* p. 52.

ROMAN Catholic controversialists assure us that there can never be a time of confusion in the Church in matters of doctrine. To assert that there has been "would be, in the mouth of a Catholic, the grossest impiety."[1] How then is it that St. Basil can speak thus in his work on the Holy Spirit (xxx. 77)?—

"Is not the tempest of the Church fiercer than a storm at sea? For in it every landmark of the Fathers has been moved, and everything upon which our opinions rested, or by which they might be defended, has been convulsed. . . . The harsh clamour of disputatious combatants, inarticulate cries, and the confused sounds of perpetual tumults, which end in the destruction of godly orthodoxy, have now filled nearly the whole Church. . . . Every one is a theologian, even the man whose soul is branded with countless pollutions. Hence revolutionists easily augment their numbers, while self-appointed individuals, with a keen appetite for place, reject the dispensation of the Holy Spirit, and then divide among themselves the high offices of the Church. . . . The lust of power is followed by a widespread and prevalent disregard of all authority, and the exhortations of superiors become absolutely null and void, for every one, in his ignorant pride, thinks he is more bound to command than to obey."

Moreover, it was the authorities of the church themselves who were in confusion." "We define creeds," writes St. Hilary, "by the year or by the month, and then we repent of our definitions, and repenting afresh we defend them,

[1] Father Richardson's *What are the Catholic Claims?* Kegan Paul, 1889, p. 60.

and then again we anathematize those we have defended." In a word, through all this period, "the faith of the Church was subjected to assault from the Bishops," and was only saved by the faithful laity.[1]

IV

THE COMMON DIFFUSION OF THE SCRIPTURES AMONG CHRISTIANS OF THE EMPIRE. *Cf.* p. 69.

FATHER Richardson (*l.c.* p. 71) assures his readers that "to an educated man who knows what a Bible must have been in Patristic days—its enormous size and exceeding costliness —to take *au pied de lettre* the exhortations of a St. Gregory or a St. Chrysostom to his hearers to search diligently the Scriptures, cannot but provoke a smile." On the contrary "an educated man" knows that books in the Roman Empire were exceedingly cheap. The exceeding low price of books at Rome, says Dean Merivale, "shows that the labour (of transcription) must have been much less and much cheaper than we usually imagine." (One book of Martial, he mentions, could be got for 4d.) Thus "they were within the reach of quite poor people, . . . and the poor fellow whom Juvenal describes as 'living in a garret' had a small collection of books."[2] A similar state of things prevailed among the educated classes of the Roman Empire generally

Thus we should have supposed on general grounds that the "Sacred Scriptures" would be quite common among the Christians, and we actually have the following luminous passages on the subject in St. Chrysostom's homilies : "There is another excuse (for not reading the Bible) employed by persons of an indolent frame of mind, which is utterly devoid of reason, namely, that they do not possess books. Now, as far as the wealthy are concerned, it would

[1] Hilary *ad Constant.* ii. 5, 1-8. See Newman, *Arians of the Fourth Century.* App. note V.
[2] Merivale *Romans under the Empire* vi. p. 408 (ed. 1876). Gow *Companion to School Classics* (Macmillan) p. 23.

be ridiculous to spend words on such a pretext. But as, I believe, many of our poorer brethren are in the habit of using it, I should be glad to ask them the question, Have they not every one got complete and perfect the tools of their respective trades, be the hindrance of poverty never so great? Is it not a shame then if you make no excuse of poverty in such a case, but take care that no impediment shall interfere with you, and in this matter, where such immense benefit is to be reaped, you whine about your want of leisure and your poverty!" "Though hunger pinch men, though poverty afflict them, they will prefer to endure all hardships rather than part with any of the implements of their trade, and live by the sale of them. Many have chosen rather to borrow for the support of their families than give up the smallest of the tools of their trade. And very naturally; for they know that if these be gone, their whole means of livelihood are lost. Now, just as the implements of their trade are the anvil and hammer and pincers, so the implements of our profession are the books of the apostles and prophets and all the scriptures composed by Divine inspiration, very full of profit. As with the implement they fashion whatever vessels they take on hand, so we with ours labour at our own souls, and correct what is injured and repair what is worn out."[1]

V

DOUBTS EXPRESSED AS TO THE NATURE OF THE DOCUMENT ON ABYSSINIAN ORDERS, CITED ABOVE, pp. 150 *ff.*

THIS document has been recently called by *The Tablet* a "bogus document." It was cited by me from the best of recent Roman Catholic divines writing against our orders. But an (otherwise singularly evasive) letter of Cardinal Patrizi, secretary to the Holy Office, written to Cardinal Manning in 1875,[2] asserts that "it was not a decree of the

[1] *Chrysost.* Opp. (ed. Bened.) vol. viii. p. 63; vol. i. p. 736. Quoted by Salmon *Infallibility* pp. 118-19.
[2] *De hierarch.* p. 248.

Sacred College as appears from its records." What it was, he does not say, but recently it has been suggested that it was a (rejected) "votum" of one or more "consultors." Surely, however, if it had been only this, Patrizi would have said so. As it is, in simply saying that it was not a decree, he suggests to one's mind the idea that it may have been something one stage removed from it. (Estcourt, whom I quoted, had not called it a decree, but a resolution.) Supposing, however, that it was only a "votum" in 1704, what *was* the resolution issued at that time? And further, what is to be said against the fact that in 1860 it was cited as authoritative in the reply sent by the Holy Office to a fresh enquiry of the Vicar Apostolic for the Copts in the case of two monophysite priests who desired to be received into the Roman Church, and was described in this reply as (not a decree, but) "a resolution of the S. O., given feria iv. 9. April 1704"? It must have had the authority of the S. O. at least on this later occasion, and was certainly acted upon by the Vicar Apostolic as authoritative.[1] Meanwhile, as the matter is still under discussion, and we clearly have not got to the bottom of the matter, it is important to remark that the argument for the validity of our "form" of ordination, does not in any way depend upon the character of this document. This is apparent in the convincing argument of Fr. Puller's tract on *The Bull Apostolicae Curae*, or of *The Treatise on the Bull* (Ch. Hist. Soc.) referred to above cap. xi. The very various rites of ordination accepted in the Catholic Church at different times do not allow us to suppose anything more to be essential to the "form" or "matter" of ordination than the laying on of a bishop's hands accompanied by some imperative or precatory formula which implies the intention to ordain to the particular office. This intention is in the Anglican ordinal abundantly clear, and we have both a precatory and an imperative formula both in the ordination of bishops and of priests.

[1] This appears in his letter to Estcourt; see Denny and Lacey *De hierarch.* p. 246; see also Mr. Lacey's letter in *Tablet*, December 19, 1896, p. 983, and cf. *Revue Anglo-Romaine*, T. i. p. 369 ff.

www.ingramcontent.com/pod-product-compliance
Lightning Source LLC
Chambersburg PA
CBHW051049160426
43193CB00010B/1115